10

MINUTE GUIDE TO

NOVELL
GROUPWISE 5

by Scott Kunau

A Division of Macmillan Computer Publishing
201 West 103rd St., Indianapolis, Indiana 46290 USA

To Kelly and Sam: The two brightest lights in my life who inspire me to be the very best every day.

©1997 by Que® Corporation

International Standard Book Number: 0-7897-0726-8
Library of Congress Catalog Card Number: 95-72602

99 98 97   8 7 6 5 4 3 2 1

Interpretation of the printing code: the rightmost double-digit number is the year of the book's first printing; the rightmost single-digit number is the number of the book's printing. For example, a printing code of 97-1 shows that this copy of the book was printed during the first printing of the book in 1997.

Printed in the United States of America

Publisher Roland Elgey

Publishing Manager Lynn E. Zingraf

Editorial Services Director Elizabeth Keaffaber

Managing Editor Michael Cunningham

Director of Marketing Lynn E. Zingraf

Acquisitions Editor Martha O'Sullivan

Technical Specialist Nadeem Muhammed

Product Development Specialist Melanie Palaisa

Technical Editor Sandy Hagman

Production Editor Tom Lamoureux

Book Designer Barbara Kordesh

Cover Designer Dan Armstrong

Production Team Kim Cofer, Tricia Flodder, Janelle Herber, Megan Wade, Pamela Woolf

Indexer C. J. East

WE'D LIKE TO HEAR FROM YOU!

As part of our continuing effort to produce books of the highest possible quality, Que would like to hear your comments. To stay competitive, we *really* want you, as a computer book reader and user, to let us know what you like or dislike most about this book or other Que products.

You can mail comments, ideas, or suggestions for improving future editions to the address below, or send us a fax at (317) 581-4663. For the online inclined, Macmillan Computer Publishing has a forum on CompuServe (type **GO QUEBOOKS** at any prompt) through which our staff and authors are available for questions and comments. The address of our Internet site is **http://www.mcp.com/que** (World Wide Web).

In addition to exploring our forum, please feel free to contact me personally to discuss your opinions of this book: I'm **73353, 2061** on CompuServe, and I'm **mpalaisa@que.mcp.com** on the Internet.

Although we cannot provide general technical support, we're happy to help you resolve problems you encounter related to our books, disks, or other products. If you need such assistance, please contact our Tech Support department at 800-545-5914 ext. 3833.

To order other Que or Macmillan Computer Publishing books or products, please call our Customer Service department at 800-835-3202 ext. 666.

Thanks in advance—your comments will help us to continue publishing the best books available on computer topics in today's market.

Melanie Palaisa
Product Development Specialist
Que Corporation
201 W. 103rd Street
Indianapolis, Indiana 46290
USA

CONTENTS

INTRODUCTION

Welcome to the *10 Minute Guide to Novell GroupWise 5* and to the fastest growing electronic messaging system in the industry. Novell GroupWise 5 (referred to as GroupWise 5 throughout the rest of this book) provides you with the software tools to send and receive e-mail messages, tasks, notes, phone messages, and even appointments. You can control an extensive calendar/scheduling system, store documents, and share information easily, with just a few keystrokes or mouse clicks.

As the industry speeds forward, terms like GroupWare and Universal Inbox will appear in many software programs. GroupWise 5 provides one of the best GroupWare solutions and the only true Universal Inbox for you to send and receive information from many sources.

WHY YOU SHOULD READ THE *10 MINUTE GUIDE TO NOVELL GROUPWISE 5*

The *10 Minute Guide to Novell GroupWise 5* is a handy, easy to understand, step-by-step reference book that new users can use to become quickly proficient with GroupWise 5. This book, while small, makes the perfect reference for walking you through a particular task, whether it be to send a message, create an appointment, or view your calendar.

You can start at Lesson 1 and work through to Lesson 22 or you can jump around to pick up just the necessary tips and techniques you require.

Each lesson starts with a quick summary of what you will learn. You then proceed through several step-by-step tasks to become proficient with the lesson. Where appropriate, you will see pointers, called *Plain English, TimeSaver Tips,* and *Panic Buttons* to call attention to a definition, a quick tip, or a warning.

CONVENTIONS USED IN THIS BOOK

Specific conventions in this book help you to easily find your way around GroupWise 5:

What you type	appears in **bold, color** type
What you select	appears in color type
Menu, Field, and Key names	appear with the first letter capitalized

TERMS AND NOTES

Throughout the *10 Minute Guide to GroupWise 5,* we have included definitions, extra notes, and warnings where they fit. These are in place to help the reader understand terms and be aware of problems before they occur. The following icons are used to call your attention to this extra information.

Plain English   Definitions for terms you may not be familiar with.

TimeSaver Tip   Once you become comfortable with the features of GroupWise 5, start implementing TimeSaver Tips. Using them will make you work faster and help you avoid confusing steps.

Panic Button This icon identifies areas where you may run into trouble or where something must be set up before the task at hand will work.

FOR MORE INFORMATION...

GroupWise 5 is a Microsoft Windows 95, NT Workstation, and Windows 3.1x software program. While it will run on other platforms, such as Macintosh and Unix, we have written this book for Windows 95 and Windows NT Workstation 4.0 versions only. If the reader has a basic understanding of one of these versions of Windows, then there should be no problems working with GroupWise 5.

If you are using Windows 3.1x, GroupWise 5 will operate almost identically to GroupWise 4.1. In fact, the Windows 3.1x version looks just like GroupWise 4.1. You will unfortunately lose many of the exciting features that are part of the Windows 95 and NT 4.0 version but you will not be forced to upgrade your Windows workstation in order to begin working with GroupWise 5. If you need assistance using the Windows 3.1x version of GroupWise 5, or are looking at a publication similar to this book, we strongly suggest obtaining the *10 Minute Guide to GroupWise* written by Kate Miller. Kate's book is available from Que and covers GroupWise 4.1. It will help you become familiar with the features that are available in the Windows 3.1x version of GroupWise 5.

If you are new to both Windows and GroupWise 5, we have included a Microsoft Windows primer section in the Appendix of this book, which addresses Windows 95 and Windows NT 4.0 features. If, after reviewing the Appendix, you would like additional information about running Windows, consider purchasing and using the *10 Minute Guide to Windows 95*.

ACKNOWLEDGMENTS

This is the first book I have ever written and believe me it was a lot harder and more time consuming than I ever thought possible. The staff at Que has been incredibly generous in dealing with my schedule to get this book done as close to the release of GroupWise 5 as possible. I would like to thank Martha O'Sullivan, Acquistions Editor, for offering this project to me; Melanie Palaisa, Production Development Specialist, for working with every word I wrote to make this a great book; Tom Lamoureux, Production Editor, for having patience and working more than overtime when we came down to the wire; Sandy Hagman, Technical Editor, for making sure I have been accurate with every step; and all of the other staff members at Que who in one way or another had a part in making this book a success. Thanks to my peers who have helped me become so proficient with GroupWise and networking.

Most importantly, I must thank my wife Kelly and my son Sam for the love, support, and inspiration they provide me each and every day. Thank you both for giving me all of the time I needed to complete this book.

TRADEMARKS

All products mentioned in this *10 Minute Guide* are known or suspected to be trademarks or service marks. Where used, these products have been appropriately capitalized. Que cannot attest to the accuracy of this information. Use of a term in this book should not be regarded as affecting the validity of any trademark or service mark.

STARTING AND EXITING GROUPWISE 5

In this chapter you'll learn how to start and exit the GroupWise 5 program. You'll also take a quick tour of all the GroupWise 5 mailbox features.

The GroupWise 5 program is an application that runs best in the Windows 95 environment. (It will also run well in the Windows NT Workstation 4.0 environment and there is a Windows 3.1 version for those who haven't yet upgraded.)

 Slow Down? If you need a refresher on Windows 95 or Windows NT 4.0, check out the primer in the Appendix.

The program you are about to work with is called the GroupWise Client. It is a powerful software program; one of the best electronic messages programs in the industry today. Your GroupWise system administrator has installed GroupWise 5 onto your PC. Now it is up to you to learn how to start the program, use its most popular features, and close the program when you are done.

 Fast Tip It is usually best to run the GroupWise 5 client continuously so that your e-mail will be just a click away. Just remember to close the program when your work is finished.

STARTING THE PROGRAM

Once your PC is running, you need to find the GroupWise 5 icon on your desktop or in the program folder your system administrator created.

 If your system administrator created a shortcut to GroupWise 5, double-click the GroupWise 5 icon on the desktop to start the program. You can also click the **Start** button on the Windows task bar, click **Programs**, then click the GroupWise 5 program folder, then click on the GroupWise 5 program icon.

 Remote Mode   GroupWise 5 will automatically put itself into remote mode if you are not connected to your company's network. We'll examine GroupWise Remote in Lesson 17.

The GroupWise 5 installation program creates a folder on your Windows 95 desktop and places four different program icons into it so you can start the GroupWise 5 program by first double-clicking the folder to open it and then double-clicking the GroupWise 5 icon. See Figure 1.1.

The GroupWise 5 Client should start. If it doesn't, record the error number and contact your system administrator. The first time you start GroupWise 5, you may be asked for either your Network ID or your GroupWise 5 user ID. If so, enter the requested ID in the appropriate dialog box. The GroupWise 5 Mailbox window is displayed, as shown in Figure 1.2.

FIGURE 1.1   The GroupWise 5 program group folder.

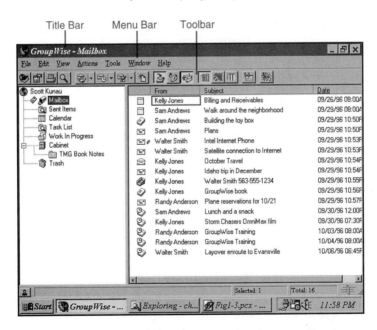

FIGURE 1.2   The GroupWise 5 main screen (your mailbox).

VIEWING THE GROUPWISE 5 MAILBOX

You have successfully launched GroupWise 5 and you wonder what to do next. The main screen includes your mailbox, a title bar, menu bar, and several icons in the GroupWise 5 toolbar located below the menu bar. In the left pane of the screen are several icons and folders, which are described later in this lesson. Initially, you should also see message items in your mailbox that others have sent to you in the right pane of the screen.

USING THE MENU BAR

The Menu bar houses all the commands available to you in GroupWise 5. You access these commands by clicking a menu command, such as the Find or Edit command. Let's look at several of the major menu commands you will find in the menu bar. We'll define the major menu command (i.e. File Menu) and then briefly explain some of the commands you will regularly use.

- **File Menu**   This menu is standard in all Windows programs. Use this menu to send new messages, to share folders, to import documents, to save and print messages, and to exit GroupWise 5.

- **Edit Menu**   This menu is standard in all Windows programs. From the Edit menu you can copy and paste text and graphics from one program to another. For example, in GroupWise 5 you may want to copy a paragraph from a document into a mail message. Specific GroupWise 5 commands include the capability to empty your trash (see Lesson 7) and convert items in your mailbox to another type of item (a mail message to a task or a task to a calendar item).

- **Folders**   You will use this command to access the Folders dialog box. (See Lesson 8 to learn all about GroupWise 5 folders).

- **View Menu**   Commands in the View Menu allow you to look at your GroupWise 5 mailbox or items contained in it in a variety of ways. These include: messages, message threads, and the calendar.

- **Action Menu**   You can use the commands in the Action Menu to take action on a particular message without actually opening it. These include: reply, forward, delegate, delete, and so on.

- **Tools Menu**   There are a number of additional programs that come with GroupWise 5 and these are found in the Tools menu. For example:

    The **Address Book** is automatically launched (it automatically runs) whenever you prepare to address a message (see Lesson 9).

    The **Conversation Place** helps you set up phone calls, using telephone numbers stored in your address book. In order to use the Conversation Place, you must have a modem on your computer and be connected to a phone line (see Lesson 16).

    The **Busy Search** feature allows you to access the calendars of everyone in your company or workgroup who uses GroupWise 5 to schedule their appointments. You can locate free times on your coworkers' schedules before scheduling a meeting. (See Lessons 10 and 11 for more about appointments and your calendar.)

    The **Rules** command lets you create rules that will automate the way you handle different kinds of messages you receive or send. (See Lesson 20 on using rules.)

    Internet   This command will let you create Internet Web page addresses and place them into your cabinet or other folder on the main GroupWise 5 screen. Use this command to send a message to another user specifying an Internet Web page address. If you receive a message sent using the special Internet view, you can access that World Wide Web page or an Internet address directly from GroupWise 5 (see Lesson 18).

    Options   You can customize GroupWise 5 using this command. You can set a password, set up send options, and control your GroupWise 5 defaults for views and cleanup options.

Window Menu   This menu is standard in all Windows programs. Commands let you open a different view of your mailbox, close a view, and minimize the program. If multiple views are open, you can use the Window menu to switch to another view.

Help Menu   This menu is standard in all Windows programs. Commands let you access the GroupWise 5 help system. You can access the help topics for a list of all commands, access GroupWise Guides (short tutorials on common tasks) and access the Novell homepage on the Internet (see Lesson 2 for more about using Help).

USING THE TOOLBAR

Instead of using menu commands for every GroupWise 5 operation, try using a Toolbar button. Using a button is an effective way to access a menu command like Create a new mail message/appointment/ or task; you can also use a Toolbar button to change the overall view of your mailbox, and much more. If you are unsure what a particular button does, simply move your mouse onto the button to see a short description or "tooltip" appear.

Toolbar   The icon bar located across the top of your GroupWise 5 screen, just below the menu bar. The Toolbar includes "buttons" that access regularly used commands. You can also access these commands from the Menu bar.

FIGURE 1.3   The GroupWise 5 Toolbar.

AN INTRODUCTION TO GROUPWISE 5 FEATURES

As you saw in Figure 1.2, the left pane of the GroupWise 5 mailbox screen (under the toolbar) contains several icons and folders that allow you to access other features of GroupWise 5. Here is a summary, in top-down order, of what these features are:

- **Mailbox** The folder where received messages are located.

- **Sent Items** This folder holds all of the messages that you send to others.

- **Calendar** This item allows you to display your calendar. You can view your daily schedule, reminder notices, and tasks assigned to you by clicking on the Calendar. You learn more about using the Calendar in Lessons 10 through 13.

- **Task List** This folder shows all of your tasks, regardless of where in your mailbox they may actually be located (i.e. mailbox, cabinet, trash). (See Lesson 14 for more about the task list.)

- **Work In Progress** This folder is for storing messages that you are not finished composing. It will also display documents you recently worked on and saved via the GroupWise 5 Document Management System.

- **Cabinet** The Cabinet serves as a holder for your personal folders (see Lesson 8 for more on folders). You should use the Cabinet to create folders to help organize your mailbox.

- **Trash** The trash folder holds message items that you have deleted from the other folders of your mailbox. Lesson 7 explains more about the Trash folder.

You may find messages in each of your mailbox folders. In the next lesson we will learn how to open a message, read it and reply, or take other action on it.

UNDERSTANDING THE GROUPWISE 5 MESSAGE TYPES

You will see different types of messages in the right pane of your GroupWise 5 mailbox. Table 1.1 explains what the different message types are:

TABLE 1.1   GROUPWISE MAIL MESSAGE TYPES

THIS ICON...	REPRESENTS...
	Normal mail messages. The closed envelope means you have not read the message
	Phone messages
	A note (either read or new)
	A message sent to you that requires a response
	A red message means it was sent as a high-priority message
	An appointment (opened and unopened)
	A task (opened and unopened)
	A message with an attachment

EXITING GROUPWISE 5

At the end of the day, you should exit GroupWise 5 instead of simply turning your computer off. By exiting the software, you allow GroupWise 5 to perform normal shutdown and maintenance procedures. In doing so, you help to prevent system problems with your mailbox. To exit the GroupWise 5 mailbox, do one of the following:

- Click on the File menu and choose the Exit command.

- Click once on the control menu in the upper-left corner of the GroupWise 5 screen and choose the close command.

- Press Alt+F4 to quickly exit GroupWise 5 and return to the main Windows 95 desktop.

In this lesson you learned how to start GroupWise 5, look at each of the different mailbox folders and then exit the program. In the next lesson you will learn how to use the GroupWise 5 help system.

2

USING THE GROUPWISE 5 HELP SYSTEM

In this lesson you'll learn how to use the various types of online help provided by GroupWise 5.

No one likes to read the long technical manuals written on the software you use, looking for a few simple keystrokes to achieve a task in the software. That is a major reason why online help is available in nearly every software program available today. GroupWise 5 is no exception. There are several different ways to access topics in the GroupWise 5 help system.

USING HELP CONTENTS

The Help Contents tab in the Help Topics dialog box provides an alphabetical listing of all the topics in the GroupWise 5 help system. This is probably a good place to look when you're learning new features about the program or you have a general topic you want more information on. Follow these steps to learn how to locate information using the Help Contents tab:

1. Open the GroupWise 5 main program. Select Help, Help Topics from the menu. In the Help dialog box (see Figure 2.1) click the Contents tab if it is not already selected. Each Help topic has a closed book icon to the left of it.

2. Double-click a closed "book" icon to display information about the topic. Depending on the help topic, you may see more closed books, indicating there are additional help topics, or you may see a document icon with a question mark on it. Double-click the document icon to read a description of that particular help topic.

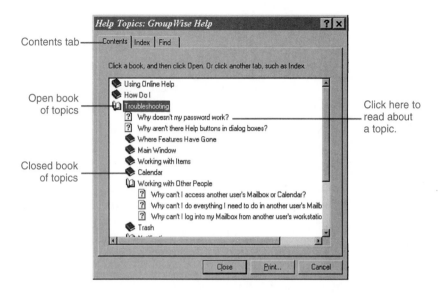

FIGURE 2.1   The Help Topics for GroupWise 5.

Once the help topic is displayed on the screen (see Figure 2.2), use the buttons on the toolbar to navigate through the help system and change options:

- The Help Topics button allows you to return to the Help Topics Contents screen to choose another topic or close the Help feature.

- The Back button lets you access previous Help topics you've read in the current session. If the displayed topic is the first topic you've viewed in this session, the Back button is dimmed.

- The Option button allows you to do several things:

    Annotate   Lets you add your own information to a help topic. A paper clip will appear if you annotate a help topic.

    Copy   Copy the topic to the Windows clipboard to paste it into another application.

Print Topic   Lets you print the help topic.

Font   Choose the display font for the help topic.

Keep Help On Top   Lets you keep the help screen on top of all other windows so you can refer to the help steps without having to cycle back to the help topic screen.

Use System Colors   Lets you change the color of the help screen to the same color your windows system is using.

Open a File   Lets you open another help topic file, without going back to the contents screen.

Exit   Leaves the help system.

Define a Bookmark   Lets you place a reference mark in a help topic so you can return to it quickly, without having to search for the topic again.

Display a Bookmark   Displays a list of your current bookmarks.

Version   Displays the current version of the help system.

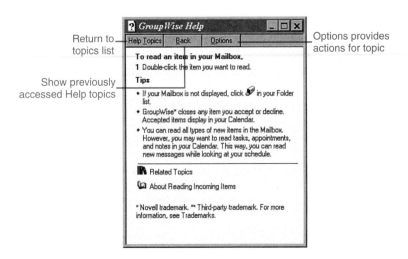

FIGURE 2.2   Specific GroupWise 5 Help Topic.

USING THE GROUPWISE 5 HELP INDEX

Often, the easiest way for you to find help on a particular topic is to use the Index. Rather than choosing the Contents tab and trying to figure out in which "book" the command you need help with appears, you can use the Index and scroll through the list of commands. Better yet, typing a word or two will automatically scroll to the topic you type, if it exists in the Index. Follow these steps to open and use the Help Index.

1. Choose Help, Help Topics from the menu. In the Help Topics dialog box, click the Index tab to display its contents, if it's not in front (see Figure 2.3).

FIGURE 2.3   The GroupWise 5 Help Index.

2. Type the first few letters of the topic you need to search for in the **1. Type the first few letters of the word you're looking for** text box. As you type, the list under **2. Click the index entry you want, and then click Display** area scrolls and selects a possible match to the words you typed in the text box.

3. Click the index entry you want, then click Display to read the topic. Depending on the topic selected, you may need to select from additional sub-lists to locate the desired topic.

CONTEXT-SENSITIVE HELP

GroupWise 5 provides help on nearly all buttons, boxes, commands, and screens you will encounter. For example, if you have a question about a particular command in a dialog box, you can use context-sensitive help by pressing the F1 key. The location of your cursor or mouse in the dialog box will determine what context-sensitive help screen appears. Usually the context help appears in a small window and offers one to four short sentences. Follow these steps to access context-sensitive help:

1. Select a GroupWise 5 command from the menu bar. A window similar to the one in Figure 2.4 will open. (Figure 2.4 shows the Rules dialog box that appeared after choosing the **Tools** menu and the **Rules** command.)

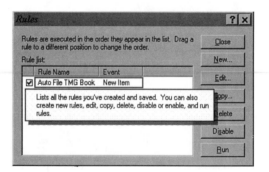

FIGURE 2.4   An example of context-sensitive help.

2. Position your mouse cursor on or near the command, button, or box you need help with and press the F1 key on your keyboard.

3. When you are done reading the short help explanation, click your mouse elsewhere on the screen. The help screen will disappear so you can continue working.

IN OTHER WORDS...

One of the hardest parts to learning a software program is figuring
out what the software company calls all of its features. If you
don't know what the feature is called, but you know what you
would like to accomplish, you can use the **In Other Words**
command in the GroupWise 5 help system. This command is
found under the Help menu. Follow these steps to access In Other
Words:

1. Choose In Other Words from the Help menu. The In
    Other Words dialog box appears as seen in Figure 2.5.

2. Type a word or words of a GroupWise 5 topic that you
    want to know about into the **What do you want to
    know?** box.

3. Select the Search button to cause GroupWise 5 to match,
    as closely as it can, any help topic that resembles what
    you typed.

4. If you find the topic in the **Click the item, then click
    the display button** list box, select the item and click
    on the Display button to display that topic.

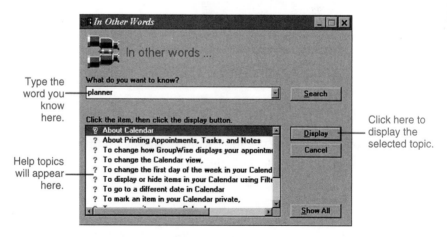

FIGURE 2.5   The In Other Words dialog box.

GROUPWISE GUIDES

The last type of help available for GroupWise 5 comes in the form of Guides. GroupWise Guides are a form of step-by-step helpers that will lead you through a simple or a complex task. Follow these steps to access GroupWise Guides.

1. Choose the Help menu and click on the Guides command. The GroupWise Guides dialog box appears as seen in Figure 2.6.

Major topics   Specific topics Screen prompt Close Guides screen

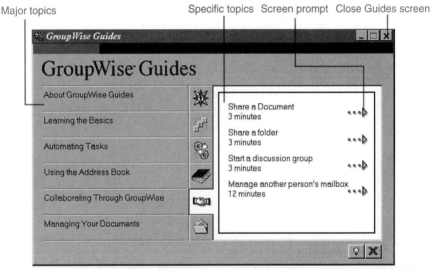

FIGURE 2.6   GroupWise Guides.

2. In the center of the GroupWise Guides dialog box, you will see six icons. These represent major topics. Click once on one of the major topic icons to show a list of subjects that will be covered by that topic.

3. A list of specific topics appears on the right side of the GroupWise Guides dialog box. Choose the specific topic you would like to review by clicking on one of the arrows to the right of the topic. Each topic appears with its estimated completion time.

4. Navigate through the guide lesson by clicking on the arrow pointing to the right, when prompted (see Figure 2.7). At the end of the guide, you can return to the main screen by clicking on the star icon, or you can exit the guide by clicking on the red X icon.

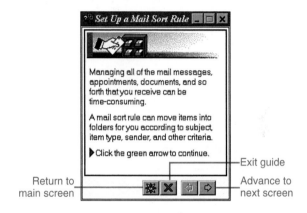

FIGURE 2.7   A GroupWise Guide Specific topic.

In this lesson you learned about the different ways to activate and use GroupWise 5 help. In the next lesson you will learn how to open and read GroupWise 5 messages.

LESSON 3

READING MAILBOX ITEMS

In this lesson you will learn how to open, read, save, print, and delete mail and phone messages in your GroupWise 5 mailbox.

We have all received piles of those pink phone messages and piles of memos and other mail. Managing all of this paper can sometimes be overwhelming. GroupWise 5 offers you a variety of message types to help you manage information. These include mail and phone messages, tasks, appointments, notes, and documents.

OPENING AND READING MAIL AND PHONE MESSAGES

After starting the GroupWise 5 program, which you learned to do in Lesson 1, you are automatically presented with your mailbox. You will see opened and unopened messages as well as the various folders discussed in Lesson 1.

We will use only mail and phone messages in this lesson—tasks, notes, and appointments will be covered in Lessons 11 and 12.

To read a mail or phone message, simply double-click it. The GroupWise 5 message should appear on the screen, as shown in Figure 3.1.

 TIP   **The Quick Menu**   You can right-click almost anywhere on the GroupWise 5 screen to bring up a quick menu that will offer a variety of different commands to you, depending upon the area or item you right-click on. This helps you avoid accessing the menu bar for every command.

Quick Menu   A pop-up menu that lists a specific set of items that apply to a particular feature. You open a Quick Menu by pointing to a message and then pressing the right mouse button. Then click the left mouse button on the command you want.

The message is
from this user

To: identifies
the recipient

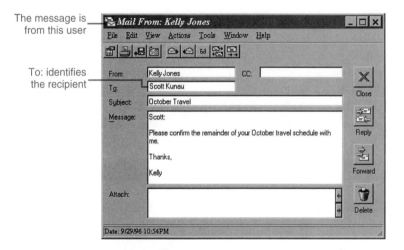

FIGURE 3.1   An opened GroupWise 5 message.

You are given several options when you open a message: You can reply, forward, print, save, or delete the message. You can also open the next or previous message in your mailbox from this screen by pressing Ctrl + the down arrow or Ctrl + the up arrow.

PRINTING AND SAVING MESSAGES

You can save or print messages received in your mailbox:

1. Open the message you want to print or save.

 2. Click the print icon on the toolbar to print the message. The Print dialog box appears as shown in Figure 3.2.

Printer to which
message will print.

Message to print

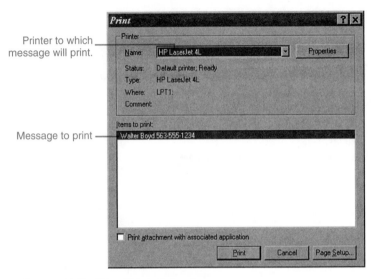

FIGURE 3.2 The Print dialog box.

3. Click the Print button to print the open message.

Printer Configuration The printer you normally print
your work to has already been configured by your system
administrator and will show up in the Name drop-down list
in the Print dialog box. You can change printers, but contact your system administrator first.

Choice of Printers? Be sure to select the correct printer
before trying to print the message. Otherwise, the message may not print properly or it may not print at all. Contact your system administrator if you are having trouble
printing messages.

4. To save an open message, click the Save button on the
toolbar. The Save dialog box is displayed, as shown in Figure
3.3.

5. The filename of the message will appear in the Save File As field. Note that the subject of the message is automatically used as the filename. You can change the filename by typing in this field.

6. By default, the directory from which GroupWise 5 runs will appear in the Current directory field. You can customize the directory that automatically appears here by customizing GroupWise 5. If you want to change the current directory, click browse and navigate to the directory where you want the message to be saved.

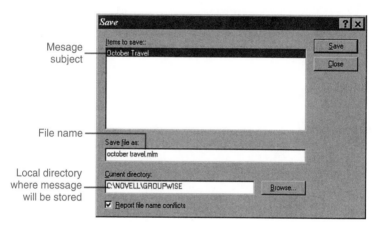

Mesage subject

File name

Local directory where message will be stored

FIGURE 3.3   The Save Message dialog box.

DELETING A MESSAGE FROM YOUR MAILBOX

Let's say you decide to delete a message from your Mailbox. This can be accomplished with keystrokes or with your mouse. You can delete a message using any one of the following methods:

- Open the message you want to delete and click the Delete button.

- Simply click the message you want to delete in the Mailbox window and press the Delete key on your keyboard.

- Right-click the message and choose Delete from the quick menu.

Recoverable Messages? If you delete messages from your mailbox, remember that until they are removed from your Trash folder, you can recover them. After the trash is emptied, messages are no longer recoverable. See Lesson 7 for more about the Trash folder.

In this lesson you learned how to open and read phone and e-mail messages. You also learned to save, print, and delete phone and e-mail messages. In next lesson, you will learn how to send messages.

CREATING AND SENDING A GROUPWISE 5 MESSAGE

In this lesson you'll learn to send mail and phone messages both in your own company and on the Internet, to address a message, and to change the send options of a mail message.

You want to send a letter but you don't want to wait for it to be delivered the conventional way or you just ran out of those pink telephone message pads. You're wondering how the person who needs to get the letter or phone message will receive it. Your answer—electronic mail. With electronic mail, you can quickly send a letter or phone message to a recipient.

CREATING A NEW MAIL MESSAGE

You can create a new mail message in several ways. One of the easiest is to use the button bar on the GroupWise 5 mailbox screen (see Figure 4.1). To *send* a message, you have three view options. In this lesson we will work with the default view.

The default view allows you to address recipients via the TO:, CC:, and BC: fields as well as include a subject line, a message, and attachments in your message. The two other view options, small mail and expanded mail, allow for variations on these items.

Press this icon to
start a new task.

Press this icon
to begin a new   Press this icon to
mail message.   begin a new note.

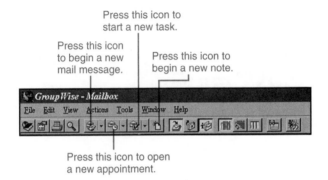

Press this icon to open
a new appointment.

FIGURE 4.1   The GroupWise 5 Mailbox button bar.

 Views   Different ways you can see information sent to you in the form of a message. There are default views for each of the GroupWise 5 message types. Each message type has other views available that can be set as a default or accessed at will. (See Lessons 11 and 12 to learn about the other message types and their specific views.)

 1. Click the Create New Mail button on the button bar or choose the File menu, the New command and then Mail. The default Mail To: dialog box is displayed as shown in Figure 4.2.

 Quick Access   You can press **Ctrl + M** to quickly access the Mail To: view.

2. Your cursor is automatically placed in the TO: box. Here you can type the address of the recipient or choose the Address button to access the GroupWise 5 Address Book. You learn more about addressing your message later in this lesson.

3. Type in the name of a GroupWise 5 user or GroupWise 5 group and press Tab.

4. **(Optional)** You can insert GroupWise 5 usernames into the CC: and BC: fields (to send the message to carbon copy and blind carbon copy recipients). Or press **Tab** to bypass the CC: box and the BC: box and move your cursor to the Subject: box.

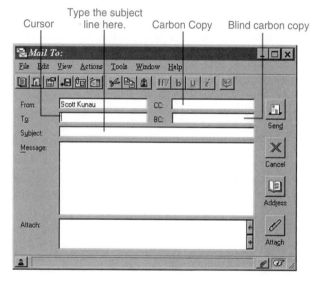

FIGURE 4.2   A new mail message ready to be addressed.

CC:, BC: Sends a copy of the message and informs other user(s) that you sent the message to the user in the TO: box. Use BC:s, or blind carbon copies, so the original recipient doesn't know the message was also sent to another user. Use CC: (carbon copy) when you want the person in the TO: box to know who else received a copy of the message.

5. Enter a short subject for your message and press Tab to move to the Message box.

6. Begin typing your message. When you are done, you can click the Send command in the Mail To: dialog box, or choose the File, Properties command and then apply send options.

Attachments   You can attach a file to your message to share information with others on GroupWise 5. You'll learn more about attaching files in Lesson 5.

ADDRESSING A MESSAGE

You can type the user's GroupWise 5 ID into the TO: field box, or better yet, use the Address Book to pick the user or group of users from a list. We will explore complete usage of the Address Book in Lesson 9. To use the Address Book, follow these steps:

GroupWise 5 User ID   The identifier your system administrator uses when you are included in the GroupWise 5 system. This ID may be your first name or a combination of letters from your first and last names. Your system administrator will likely include your first and last name so users can easily identify you when they address a message to you. While your first and last name will appear in the address book, your user ID will appear in the TO:, CC:, and BC: fields because GroupWise 5 needs this ID to deliver a message to you.

1. Start a new message and click the Address button. The Novell GroupWise 5 Address Book displays as shown in Figure 4.3. This is the "public" address book that all users will see. The other address books will be discussed in Lesson 9.

Choose the
addressee from
this list.

Click one of these buttons
to insert addressee into
your e-mail message.

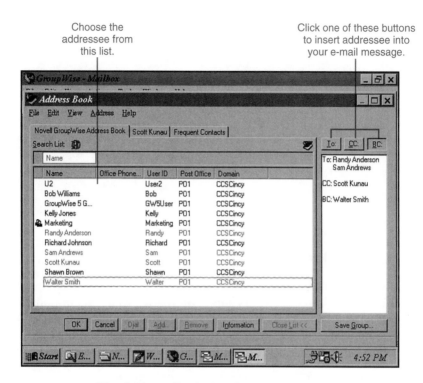

FIGURE 4.3   The Address Book showing users added to the TO:
CC: BC: box.

2. To pick an addressee from the address book, double-click
   the user name or click once and then click on one of the
   buttons in the upper-right portion of the screen (**TO: CC:
   BC:**). This adds the user to the chosen address field of the
   Mail To: view screen. You can also click once on a user ID
   and drag it to the chosen field.

3. When you have picked all of the users, public or personal
   groups and resources, that you want to send the message
   to, click the OK button. You will return to the Mail To:
   view.

Public, Personal Groups and Resources Different items that may appear in the address book. A public group or distribution list is created by your system administrator and includes the entire department, for example. A personal group is one you create that will include a group of people you frequently send messages to. A resource is also created by the system administrator and represents rooms and equipment that can be scheduled or checked out via a GroupWise 5 message.

UNDERSTANDING GROUPWISE 5 SEND OPTIONS

You can choose from many options before sending a message through the GroupWise 5 system. You change your send options in the Mail and Phone Properties dialog box shown in Figure 4.4. Here are some options you can change:

- **Priority** You can change the priority of the message, which might make the message move the GroupWise 5 system quicker and will make the icon representing it change colors in the recipient's mailbox (red for high priority, for example).

- **Status information** What appears in the information screen when you view it. The options are to know if a mail message was delivered to the recipient and subsequently opened (Delivered and Opened is the default).

- **Return notification** Allows you to receive notification or a mail message indicating that the message was opened, deleted, or completed. (None is the default.)

- **Reply requested** You can request that the recipient reply to your message and set a time limit for the reply. This changes the icon that appears in the recipients' mailbox from an envelope to a double-directional arrow. The words **Reply Requested By:** and a date appear at the top of the message. The default setting is None.

- **Expiration** If you choose to Expire a message, the message will be removed after the number of days you indicate providing the recipient does not open it. This is handy for time-sensitive messages that must be handled by recipients in order to meet a deadline.

- **Auto-delete** Will delete the message from your Sent Items folder once it is deleted from every recipient's mailbox.

You can change your send options using the following steps:

1. After completing your message, but before you send it, choose the File, Properties command from the menu bar. This brings up the Mail and Phone Properties dialog box (see Figure 4.4). Remember, the changes you make here only affect the message you are about to send, whether it is a mail message or phone message.

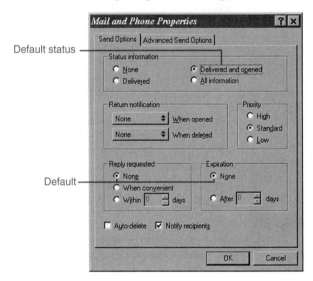

FIGURE 4.4   Mail and Phone Message Properties.

2. Make changes to any of the options described above by clicking the option (a dot or check mark indicates the option is active) or selecting the option from a drop-down list.

3. When you are finished selecting the send options for this message, click OK and then click Send to send your message. (In Lesson 21 you will learn how to change the preferences that will affect every message you send.)

SENDING AND RECEIVING A PHONE MESSAGE

Phone messages are similar to regular mail messages. You address a phone message in the same way you address a mail message, and you also read the message in the same way. You handle a phone message in the same way you work with a mail message. (See Lesson 5 on saving and printing messages; Lesson 6 on replying and forwarding messages; Lesson 7 on deleting messages; and Lesson 8 on organizing your mailbox with folders.) To send a phone message, follow these steps:

1. Choose the File menu and the New command and then choose Phone Message.

2. The default "While You Were Out" blank phone message "view" will appear on your GroupWise 5 screen (see Figure 4.5). Click the Address button to go to the Address Book to choose who you are sending the phone message to. Click OK in the Address Book once you have chosen the recipient. You can also type the name of the recipient in the TO: box.

3. Press the Tab key to move to each of the fields (Caller, Company, Phone, Message). You can change the send options for phone messages just as you did for a regular mail message. Plus, you can easily change the priority of the message by clicking on the Priority button and changing the **Standard** to either **high** or **low**. You should also check the various options specific to the phone message: **Telephoned, Please call, Will call again, Returned your call, Wants to see you, Came to see you**, and **Urgent**.

4. Click the Send button or, if you require a return receipt or
   need to change any of the other send options, choose the
   File menu and the Properties command. Click the Send
   Options tab and choose the options you need (such as
   auto-delete, return notification, priority, and so on). Click
   OK and then send the phone message.

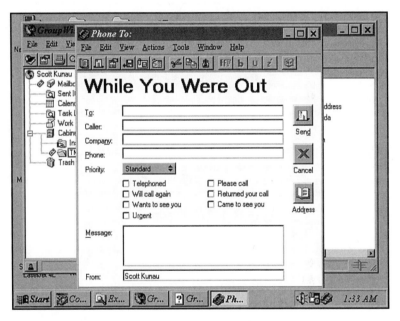

FIGURE 4.5 A blank phone message.

READING A PHONE MESSAGE

Reading a phone message is just like reading a regular mail message. The phone message will appear with a small telephone icon
next to the name column. If the phone is on the hook, the phone
message has not been opened, if it is off the hook, you have
opened the message already. Follow these steps to open and read
a phone message.

1. Click your Mailbox folder and look for any messages that
   have the telephone icon next to them. Double-click one
   of these messages to open it or right-click the message
   and choose Open from the quick menu.

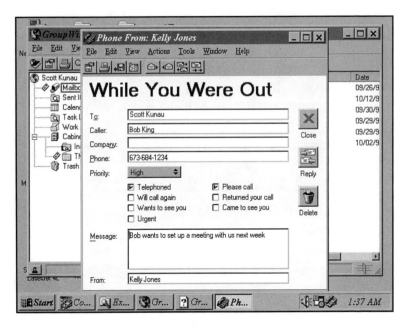

FIGURE 4.6 A received phone message.

2. You can take several types of action on a phone message, just like you can with any of the other message types. These include forwarding, replying, deleting, printing, and saving. We will examine all of these actions in Lessons 5 through 8. Once you have read the message, click the Close button to close the message.

In this lesson you learned how to open a new mail message, address the message using the address book, and change the send options for the message before sending it to a user or group of users. In the next lesson, you will learn to save and print messages and to work with attachments.

SENDING, READING, AND SAVING ATTACHMENTS

In this lesson you'll learn how to send a message with an attachment, how to view or print the attachment, and how to save an attachment that someone has sent to you.

SENDING AN ATTACHMENT

Before electronic messaging programs came along, about the only way to exchange files with other users was the "sneakernet" method. In other words, you copied a file to a diskette and then walked it over to the recipient. Now, with GroupWise 5, it is as easy to click the mouse a few times and include several attachment files with the messages you send. Follow these steps to add an attachment to a mail message:

1. Create a new mail message and address it. Your message should tell the recipient(s) what the attached files are and what to do with them.

2. Click the Attach button on the mail message view. This will take you to the Attachments dialog box (see Figure 5.1).

3. Click the Select File button. In the Attach File dialog box (see Figure 5.2), locate the file or files that will become attachments to your e-mail message and click the file(s). To select several contiguous files, select the first file then hold down the Shift key as you click on the other files. They will all be highlighted. To select several non-contiguous files, hold down the Ctrl key as you click each one.

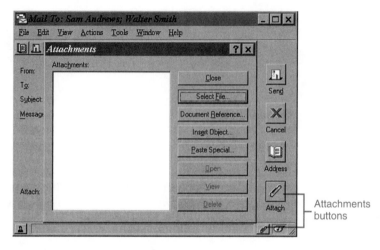

FIGURE 5.1   The Attachments dialog box.

Selected file

Current
directory

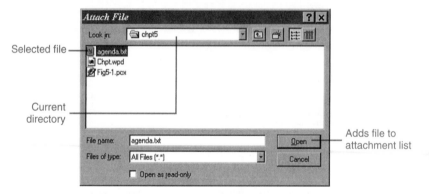

Adds file to
attachment list

FIGURE 5.2   Click one or more files in the Attach File dialog box.

 Locate Files?   If you are unsure how to search through
your file system to locate files, contact your system administrator or read through the Appendix.

4. Click Open to leave the Attach File dialog box. Notice that one or more files will appear in the Attachments box of the Attachments dialog box.

5. Click the Close button (X) in the Attachments dialog box to return to your mail message. You should see one or more files in the Attach box of your mail message (see Figure 5.3).

6. Click Send if your message is complete.

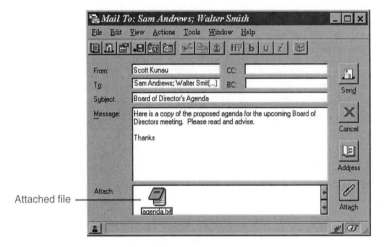

FIGURE 5.3   A Mail message with an attachment.

VIEWING/PRINTING AN ATTACHMENT

You will know an attachment is included when you see a paper clip next to the message icon in your mailbox. Before we learn how to view an attachment, you need to understand how attachment files are handled by the GroupWise 5 viewer technology.

By default, your computer has access to a comprehensive list of files to enable you to view attachments. These files are installed during the GroupWise 5 installation by your system administrator. However, as complete as this list of viewer files is, sometimes you will receive an attachment that is not supported by GroupWise 5. If this is the case, you will receive an error stating that no viewer exists. You can try to view the attachment with a substitute viewer by choosing the **Unsupported formats** command from the quick menu by right-clicking on the attachment screen. As comprehensive as the GroupWise 5 viewer technology is, this error should rarely occur.

Viewing an attachment is usually faster than trying to open the file with the application that was used to create it. See Figure 5.4 for an example of an attachment in view. To view the attachment (and perhaps print it), follow these steps.

 No Editing Shortcuts   You cannot edit attachments in a viewer. You must open the attachment using its associated application (see the task below on associated applications) in order to edit the attachment.

1. Open the message. At the bottom of the message, notice one or more attached files.

2. Use the right mouse button and click once on an attachment. You will see a quick menu appear offering the choices to View Attachment, Open, Save As, and Print. Choose View Attachment.

 Opening Attachments   In order to open an attachment you must have access to the application that was used to create it. If the extension on the attachment is not recognized by GroupWise 5, the Open With dialog box may appear asking you what application should be used to open the file. Browse through the list for the correct application, select it, and click OK.

Associated Application   A program that has been picked for use based on a file's extension. For example, WordPerfect associates to applications with .WPD extensions.

Mail message ——

Attached file ——

Text of attached file ——

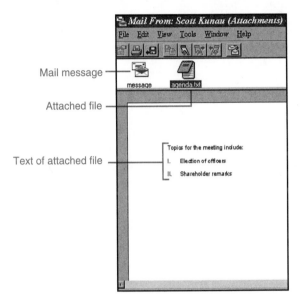

FIGURE 5.4   Viewing at attachment prior to saving or printing.

3. After viewing the attachment you can open the attachment, save or print it, or close the viewing screen:

   • To close the viewing screen and return to the message, press Alt + F4 or Esc.

   • To print the attachment from the mail message screen, right-click the attachment and choose the Print command. The Print dialog box will appear and show the various items that can be printed. Pick the attachment that you want to print and click the Print button at the bottom of the dialog box.

- To save the attachment, see the next task in this lesson.

Can't Print?   You may have trouble printing an attachment in GroupWise 5. If the attachment doesn't print correctly, open it using the associated application and then print it. If it still doesn't print properly, see your system administrator.

SAVING AN ATTACHMENT

You may want to save the attachment rather than print, view, or open it. A GroupWise 5 attachment can be opened with its associated application, provided you have that application available. Follow these steps to save the attachment to your computer's local hard drive.

1. Right-click the attachment file you want to save. Choose Save As from the Quick Menu.

2. The Save As dialog box appears (see Figure 5.5). Locate the folder in which you want to save the file, or create a new folder. You can also change the name of the file, if you want, in the File name: text box. Click the Save command to save the attachment file to your hard drive.

Save Directories   You can set a Save Directory to avoid having to browse through the file system each time you want to save an attachment or message file to your hard drive. (See Lesson 21 on GroupWise 5 options to configure a Save Directory.)

Current directory

Click here to create a new folder.

Click here to move up one level.

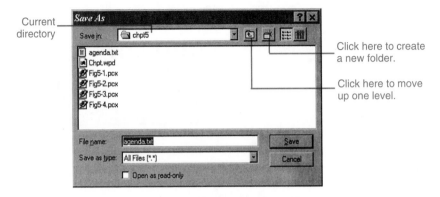

FIGURE 5.5 Preparing to save an attachment.

3. Once you have saved the attachment, you will return to the mail message, which you can now close.

In this lesson you learned how to send an attachment with a mail message, view and print an attachment, and finally how to save an attachment. In the next lesson, you'll learn how to reply, forward, and archive messages.

6

L E S S O N

REPLYING, FORWARDING, AND ARCHIVING MESSAGES

In this lesson you'll learn how to reply to messages, forward messages, and archive messages in your mailbox, and how to view discussions that are created by message replies.

MANAGING YOUR MESSAGES

Message management is critical to effectively using messaging software such as GroupWise 5. Managing messages is simply how you treat messages you send to others and messages that are sent to you, whether you reply to a message, forward it on to another person, keep the message in your mailbox for archiving, or delete it. You'll learn how to delete and handle sent messages in Lesson 7.

REPLYING TO A MESSAGE

Often when you receive a new message in your mailbox, you will want to reply to the sender, rather than create a new message from scratch. Replying to a mail message is very similar to creating a new message, except you won't have to address the message or type a subject line. You can reply to just a sender or to the sender and everyone else the message was sent to. You also have the option of including the original message in your reply. To reply to a message, follow these steps.

1. Open a mail message in your mailbox by double-clicking on it.

2. To reply to the sender, click the Reply button or choose Actions, Reply from the menu. The Reply dialog box appears as shown in Figure 6.1.

Shortcut to a Reply   You can also reply by right-clicking on a message in your mailbox and choosing the **Reply** command from the QuickMenu.

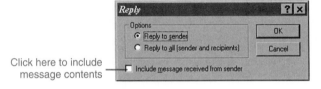

Click here to include message contents

FIGURE 6.1   The Reply dialog box.

3. Choose one of the following options:

- **Reply to sender**   Only the sender will receive your response.

- **Reply to all**   The sender and all the recipients of the message will receive your response.

You can also choose to include the original message with your response by clicking the **Include message received from sender** option to place a check mark in it. Then Click OK.

4. The Mail to: view appears similar to the one used to create the original message. Note the **Re:** in the Subject line. This indicates you are replying to the original message. Type your reply and click Send. Your reply will be sent back to the original sender and, if you checked **Reply to all**, all other recipients too.

FORWARDING A MESSAGE

Occasionally you will need to forward a message to another
GroupWise 5 user. When you forward a message to another user,
the original message is automatically sent as an attachment (see
Lesson 5 on attachments). Follow these steps to forward a message:

1. Open the message you want to forward to another user.

2. Click on the Forward button in the mail view or choose
   Actions, Forward from the menu.

 Shortcut to Forward You can also right-click the mes-
TIP sage in your mailbox and choose the Forward command
from the quick menu.

3. The message view used to create the original message will
   appear (see Figure 6.2). The original message will appear
   as an attachment and the letters **Fwd:** will appear in the
   subject line.

The original
message is
sent as an
attachment.

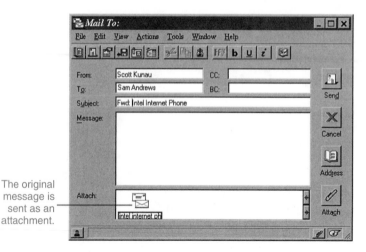

FIGURE 6.2 A mail message being forwarded.

4. Type any comments about the forwarded message in the message box and click Send.

ARCHIVING MESSAGES

The messages you and other users send and receive are kept in a central location on your network called the message store. The message store can become very large and hard to manage if you and other users don't help the system administrator maintain it by managing your own messages. You can help your system administrator manage the message store by *archiving* or pulling messages out of the message store on a regular basis. By archiving your messages, you help maintain the GroupWise 5 system and at the same time, preserve easy access to your own messages. Archiving does not destroy your messages, rather it moves them to a temporary location outside of the message store called the archive directory. This location can be placed either on your hard drive or on a network drive. Follow these steps to set up an archive location on your local hard drive.

1. Before you can start archiving messages, you must create and configure an Archive directory where your messages will be moved during the archive process. It is likely your system administrator has already done this for you, but if not, you should start from the mailbox screen and choose the Tools menu and the Options command. Click Environment and then click the Files Location tab.

2. You will need to either enter the path to your Archive Directory or use the Browse button (see Figure 6.3) and navigate through your file system to find it. If you use the Browse button, click once on it and browse to the directory you want to use for archiving. (If you are unsure how to browse through the Windows file system, read the Windows primer in the Appendix.)

3. Click OK in the Environment dialog box and then close the Options dialog box.

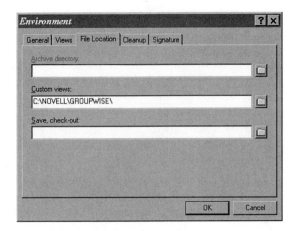

FIGURE 6.3   The File Location tab where you set your archive directory.

To Archive your messages follow these steps.

1. Open the GroupWise 5 mailbox folder where the messages to be archived are located.

2. Click on the message you want to archive and then choose the Actions menu and the Archive command. You can also use the Ctrl key and click on multiple messages to archive them at the same time.

UN-ARCHIVING MESSAGES

Remember, messages that you have archived are not destroyed, rather they are stored in a location outside the message store. However, you may at some point need to put some or all of your archived messages back into the message store so you can begin replying or forwarding them to other users. You are not required to un-archive a message if you just want to re-read or reference it. GroupWise 5 allows you to access your archived messages without un-archiving them first.

TIP

Un-archiving Once a message has been archived, it is removed from the GroupWise 5 system and placed into an archive file, on your local hard drive, or onto another drive or location on your network. By un-archiving the message, you effectively place the message back into the GroupWise 5 system.

To un-archive a message, follow these steps.

1. Choose the File menu and the Open Archive command. This opens the archive view of your mailbox.

Archive indicator

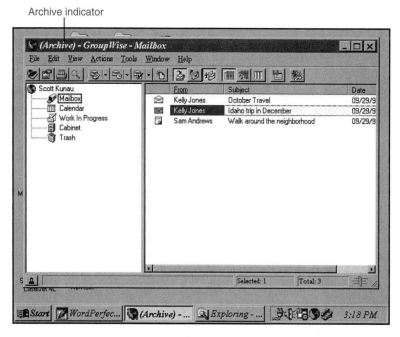

FIGURE 6.4 Archive view of your mailbox.

2. Click the folder that holds archived messages to open it.

3. Click on the message(s) you want to un-archive.

4. Choose the Actions menu and click on the Archive command to un-archive the message.

5. Finally, choose the File menu and click on the Open Archive command; this will close the archive view and return you to your GroupWise 5 mailbox.

Don't Un-archive   You can review your archived messages by following the same steps to un-archive them. However, instead of actually un-archiving them back into the message store, open and read them from your archive directory.

VIEWING DISCUSSION THREADS

New in GroupWise 5 is a feature that gives you the ability to view the subject lines of messages, connected together via replies, similar to the way messages "string" together in an online forum or newsgroup. In other words, you can see the original message and all of the replies in a single view. Each reply will appear slightly indented underneath the original message. To take advantage of this feature, you should reply to messages where possible, so messages connected together form a message thread or discussion. (See Lesson 15 on discussions.)

Discussion Thread   The initial message and all subsequent replies and responses. A discussion thread is automatically created when someone replies to a message.

In order to change the view of your mailbox so you can see discussion threads, follow these steps.

1. Select the Mailbox or other folder in the left pane of the GroupWise 5 screen by clicking once on it. (See Lesson 8 for specific information on folders.)

2. Click the View Discussion Thread button on the toolbar, or choose the View menu and the Discussion Threads command. If you have messages connected together via replies, the replies will appear indented underneath the original message. (See Figure 6.5.)

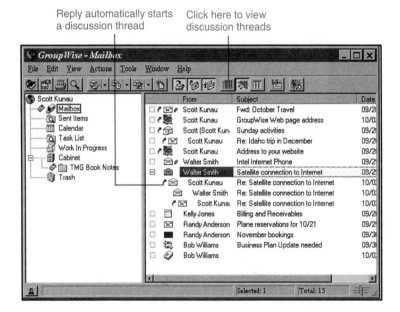

FIGURE 6.5   Messages with the arrows displaying the discussion threads.

In this lesson you learned how to reply to a message, how to forward a message, how to archive messages, and how to view discussions that are created by message replies. In the next lesson you learn how to delete messages and manage messages you have sent.

WORKING WITH THE TRASH AND SENT ITEMS FOLDERS

In this lesson you will learn how to delete messages from the folders in your mailbox, recover items from the trash, track the status of sent messages, and retract messages from recipients' mailboxes.

DELETING AND RECOVERING MESSAGES FROM THE TRASH

When you delete a message from one of the folders of GroupWise 5, it is not necessarily destroyed. By default, a message deleted in GroupWise 5 moves from a mailbox folder into the Trash folder.

You can delete a message from any mailbox folder (see Lesson 8 to learn how to use folders) by simply selecting the message and pressing the **Delete** key. You can also right-click on a message and then choose the **Delete** command from the quick menu.

To view deleted messages in the Trash folder, simply click on the Trash folder icon in the left pane of the mailbox view. The deleted items are displayed in the right pane as shown in Figure 7.1.

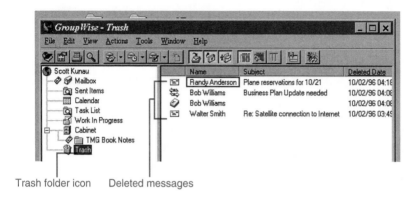

Trash folder icon   Deleted messages

FIGURE 7.1   The Trash Folder with deleted messages.

RECOVERING MESSAGES FROM THE TRASH FOLDER

After deleting a message, you may decide that you really needed to keep it for a while longer. You can recover a deleted message from the Trash folder, but you must do so before it is purged from the system (see the next section for more about purging messages from the GroupWise 5 system).

It's easy to find the message you want to keep in the Trash folder. As seen in Figure 7.1, all of the deleted messages include information about who the message was from, the subject, date of deletion, and the folder from which the message was deleted.

To recover a message, follow these steps:

1. Click the Trash folder to open it, and select a deleted message. You can right click on the message, and then choose **Undelete** from the quick menu, or you can choose the **Edit** menu and the **Undelete** command. The message will be automatically placed back into the folder it was deleted from.

A Quick Retrieval   Another way to recover messages is to simply drag them out of the Trash and place them back into the folder from which they were deleted.

Undeleting Several Messages   You can also use the **Ctrl** key and click on several messages before choosing the Undelete command rather than retrieving just one at a time.

EMPTYING THE TRASH—PURGING MESSAGES

By default, messages that have been in your Trash folder for seven days will be automatically purged. You can change this default to increase or decrease the number of days messages will be allowed to sit in your Trash folder before they are purged by the system. You can also manually empty the Trash whenever you want.

Purge   Permanently deleting messages from your Trash folder serves to remove or purge them from the GroupWise system. Once items have been emptied or purged from the Trash, they are removed from the system and are no longer recoverable. For this reason, please be cautious when emptying the Trash because purging your Trash folder results in the permanent loss of your messages.

When you empty the Trash, you are permanently removing the deleted messages, thus making them non-recoverable. To purge a single message or all messages from your Trash folder, follow these steps:

1. Open the Trash folder by clicking once on it.

2. Select a single message or a group of messages to purge and press the Delete key. You can also right-click on the message(s) and choose **Empty Selected Items** to purge just the selected messages.

3. Confirm that you want to empty the selected items by choosing Yes in the Empty Selected Items dialog box (see Figure 7.2).

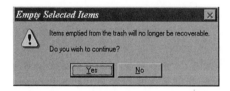

FIGURE 7.2   The Empty Selected Items dialog box.

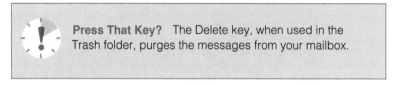

Press That Key?   The Delete key, when used in the Trash folder, purges the messages from your mailbox.

To delete *all* messages in your Trash folder, follow these steps.

1. Open the Trash folder.

2. Choose the Edit menu and the Empty Trash command. You can also right-click on a single message and choose the **Empty Trash** command from the quick menu.

3. Confirm that you want to empty all items in the trash by clicking Yes in the confirmation box (see Figure 7.3).

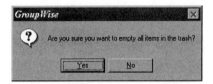

FIGURE 7.3   The Empty all items confirmation dialog box.

CHANGING PURGE OPTIONS

As mentioned earlier in the lesson, messages that you delete are located in the Trash folder until either you or the system *purge* them. By default, your GroupWise 5 software will purge messages in your Trash folder after they have been there for seven days. You or the GroupWise 5 system administrator can change this setting by following these steps:

1. Choose the Tools menu and the Options command.

2. Double-click on Environment and then choose the Cleanup tab (see Figure 7.4).

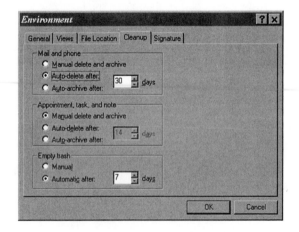

FIGURE 7.4   The GroupWise 5 Environment Options Cleanup tab.

3. Change the Empty Trash setting to an appropriate number of days and click OK. Then close the Options dialog box by either clicking on the **Close** button or clicking on the **X** button in the upper right corner of the dialog box.

How Many Days? The number of days you include in the Empty Trash setting can be based on company policy (as dictated by the GroupWise system administrator), by how many messages you receive and then delete, or how often you perform your own mailbox maintenance (cleanup, organization of messages, and so on).

TRACKING THE STATUS OF MESSAGES YOU SEND

You want to know if messages arrive and what recipients do with them, so GroupWise 5 gives you the ability to track the messages through the Sent Items folder. Each message you send is automatically copied into your Sent Items folder.

Immediately after you send a message, the first status will be **Pending**. Next, the status will change from **Pending** to **Delivered** and after that change, the next status will depend upon what message you send; whether the message has been opened; whether the task, note, or appointment is accepted or declined; or whether a message has been forwarded or delegated.

Appointments, Tasks, and Notes For more about working with Appointments, see Lesson 11. For more about tasks and notes, see Lesson 12.

Follow these steps to track the status of a message.

1. In your mailbox, click on the Sent Items folder to display all of the messages you have sent (see Figure 7.5).

2. Double-click a message to open the properties view for the selected message (see Figure 7.6). You will see the status of the message under the Action column of this view.

Sent items folder

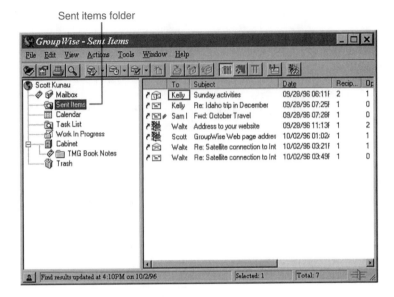

FIGURE 7.5   Your Sent Items folder.

What, No Status?   Any message you send out of your GroupWise 5 system (to the Internet or other e-mail system), will not show proper status. It is likely you will only see either a *Pending* or *Transferred* status on these messages unless the recipient system is set up to respond with a status message.

3. You can open the message to review it from the Properties screen. Choose the Open toolbar button or choose the Actions menu and the Open command to read the message.

Send It Again?   You can also resend the message, if necessary, by choosing the **Actions** menu and the **Resend** command. If you make a mistake in the message, provide wrong information, or get an undeliverable status message back, you will need to resend the message. If you resend the message, you will be prompted to retract the original message.

Open this message   Status of the message   Delivery date

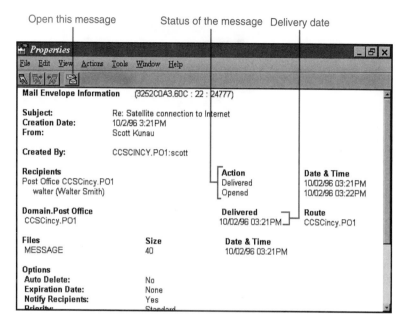

FIGURE 7.6   The message properties screen.

RETRACTING MESSAGES

If you make a mistake when sending a message, you have the option, from the message properties screen or from your Sent Items folder, to retract the message. In effect, this will remove unopened mail and phone messages or any opened or unopened task, note, or appointment messages from recipient mailboxes. To retract a message, follow these steps:

1. Open your Sent Items folder and select a message to retract.

2. Press the Delete key. This will bring up the Delete Item dialog box and offer you the opportunity to delete the message from your mailbox, from recipient mailboxes, or from all mailboxes (see Figure 7.7).

FIGURE 7.7   The Delete Item dialog box.

    Can't Retract?   You cannot retract a mail or phone mes-
sage that has been opened by the recipient. You can
retract tasks, notes, and appointments, however, that
have been opened.

3. Choose one of the following options and then click OK:

- **My Mailbox**   The message is deleted from your mailbox
  only.

- **Recipient's Mailbox**   The message is deleted from the
  recipient's mailbox only.

- **All Mailboxes**   The message is deleted from your mailbox and the recipients' mailboxes.

In this lesson you learned how to delete and recover messages
from your Trash folder, how to view the status of messages you
send, and how to retract messages you send. In the next lesson
you will learn how to create folders and use those folders to organize your mailbox.

ORGANIZING YOUR MAILBOX

LESSON

8

In this lesson you learn how to create folders in your GroupWise 5 mailbox to help you organize the messages you receive, send, and are currently creating.

Normally, you don't just throw all of your papers and files into one file cabinet drawer without first organizing the papers into file folders and then putting the file folders into some sort of organized structure. So, why should you jumble all of the messages you receive in your mailbox into one "drawer" or folder? You can use folders in all levels of your mailbox, just like you use file folders in a filing cabinet to help you sort incoming, outgoing, and personal messages.

When you use GroupWise 5 for the first time, you will see seven default folders under your user folder. The user folder represents your overall mailbox and contains all of your GroupWise 5 information. You can create additional folders under the user folder or place folders inside of other folders to further organize messages into precise subjects.

CREATING FOLDERS

You have decided to organize your GroupWise 5 mailbox and need to create several folders, based on projects you are working on; or perhaps you have decided to organize incoming messages from key people. To create a folder follow these steps:

1. Select any folder in your mailbox by clicking it and then choose Edit, Folders from the menu. The Folders dialog box appears (see Figure 8.1).

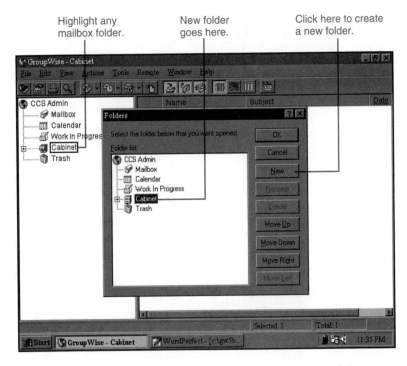

FIGURE 8.1　The Folders window shows the top levels of the mailbox.

Only in the Cabinet?　Folders can only be created inside the Cabinet or under the user folder. You cannot put one of your new folders inside one of the default folders, such as the mailbox or sent items folder. The Cabinet is also the only place you can put folders inside of each other.

2. Choose the New command. The Create Folder dialog box appears (see Figure 8.2).

3. In the Name box, type the name of your new folder.

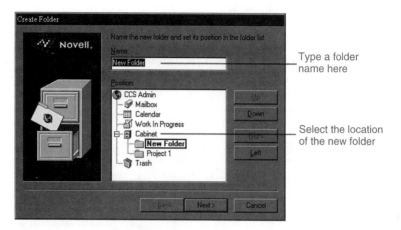

FIGURE 8.2 The Create Folder window where you name the folder.

Quick Way to a Folder   You can get to the Create Folder screen quicker by clicking once on your mailbox and pressing the mouse button on the right. The Quick Menu will appear. You should choose New Folder from this menu.

4. In the Position box, choose the Cabinet item. Your new folder will appear in the Cabinet.

5. Click Next> to move to the next screen. You can add a description for your folder (optional). Click Finish then click OK.

MOVING MESSAGES TO FOLDERS

Let's suppose you have a large number of messages in your mailbox and you have decided to move them into the folders you created in the first task.

1. In your mailbox, expand all of your folders by clicking on any plus signs (+) that you see. This way, all of your folders will appear making it easier to move messages into

them. The plus sign (+) will likely appear in the Cabinet folder only.

2. Select the message(s) you want to move out of your mailbox and into a folder you have created.

Click here to expand or
contract the cabinet

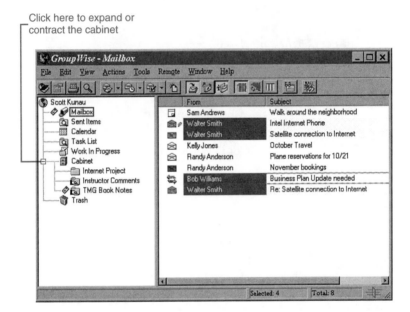

FIGURE 8.3   Selected messages ready to be moved to folders.

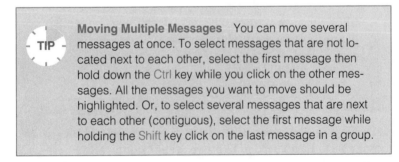

Moving Multiple Messages   You can move several messages at once. To select messages that are not located next to each other, select the first message then hold down the Ctrl key while you click on the other messages. All the messages you want to move should be highlighted. Or, to select several messages that are next to each other (contiguous), select the first message while holding the Shift key click on the last message in a group.

3. Drag the message(s) into one of the folders you have created and release the mouse button.

MOVING MESSAGES FROM FOLDERS

If you are like most people who put things in file folders and file cabinets, you know there are times when these things need to be reorganized. GroupWise 5 lets you easily reorganize messages that you have placed into folders by moving them back out into your mailbox folder or into another folder you've created. Follow these steps to move messages from a folder.

1. Click a folder to open it by clicking it once.

 Folder Not Visible?   Can't see the folder? If the folder is not showing, you will have to click on the small plus sign (+) to the left of one of the folder icons.

Click here to expand or
contract the cabinet.

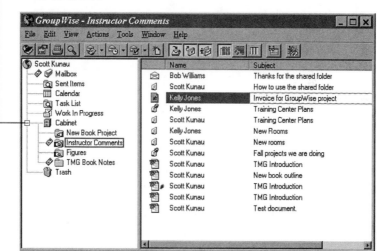

FIGURE 8.4   GroupWise Universal Inbox showing a folder underneath the Cabinet.

2. To show the messages in your folder, you need to click once on the exposed folder.

3. Select one or more messages and drag them into another folder or out into your mailbox or other default folder.

DELETING A FOLDER AND ITS CONTENTS

Let's say you have completed work on a project and now you decide to delete all messages and the special folder you made for those messages. Open a main folder by clicking on the plus sign (+). This will display any additional folders you have created and placed messages in.

1. Select the folder you want to delete.

2. Press the Delete key. The Delete Folders dialog box appears as shown in Figure 8.5.

3. To delete both the folder and all the files in it, click on the Folder(s) and Items button. Then click OK.

 Is it Gone for Good?   You don't get the opportunity to confirm the deletion of a folder and its contents so be sure you are doing the right thing before clicking OK in the Delete Folder window.

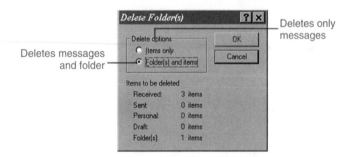

FIGURE 8.5   The Delete Folder Window shows statistics on the chosen folder.

In this chapter you learned how to create a GroupWise 5 folder, move messages into it, remove messages from it, and how to delete the folder you have created. In the next lesson, you will learn how to use the GroupWise 5 Address Book.

USING THE
ADDRESS BOOK

*In this lesson you will learn how to work
with the GroupWise 5 Address Book to
address a message, how to create a personal group
and how to add a user to your personal address book.*

THE GROUPWISE 5 ADDRESS BOOK FEATURES

The GroupWise 5 Address Book is a tightly integrated application. As an integrated application, you access the Address Book whenever you address a message. As a separate application, the Address Book allows you to keep a very detailed screen of information about your frequent business or personal contacts, just like many of the personal information manager programs available, but still access this information from GroupWise 5.

You use the Address Book to address nearly every message you send in GroupWise. When you open the Address Book dialog box (see Figure 9.1), either by clicking the Address Book icon on the toolbar or from within a new message, or by choosing **Address Book** from the **Tools** menu, you'll see as many as three default tabs, each representing a different type of address book that you can access in GroupWise 5. By default, you will see the Novell GroupWise Address Book (the public address book), a personal address book (represented by your first and last name on the tab), and a Frequent Contacts address book. You have the option to add more address books, and each would be represented by a different tab (explained later in this lesson).

You cannot add users to the Novell GroupWise Address Book because it is maintained by your system administrator; however, you can add users to both your personal and frequent contacts book as well as other address books you create.

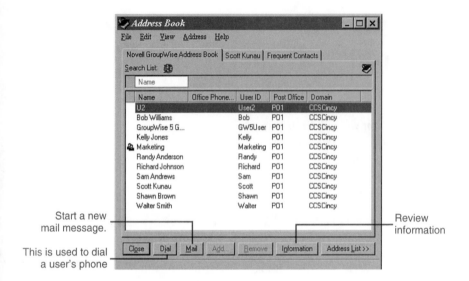

Start a new
mail message.

This is used to dial
a user's phone

Review
information

FIGURE 9.1   The GroupWise 5 Address Book.

As you learned in Lesson 4, you can use the Address Book to address a message (TO:), to send a carbon copy (CC:) or a blind carbon copy (BC:) to recipients. You can also use it as a contact manager.

CREATING A PERSONAL GROUP

In order to address messages easily, you may decide to create and keep a number of personal groups. For example, you might contact the same list of users frequently because they work with you on a project, or perhaps you supervise their daily activities. Creating a personal group saves time because you only select the group name from the address book rather than choosing each name when addressing a message.

Personal groups are not visible until you create them. You can only create them in your Frequent Contacts or Personal Address Book. Follow these steps to create a personal group:

Global Group   A group created by the system administrator for all users. A Personal Group is one that you create for your own use.

1. Open the Address Book. Click the Novell GroupWise Address Book tab, which is the System Address book, to
   bring it to the front (see Figure 9.2).

2. Select the users from the Novell GroupWise Address Book
   or from one of the other address book tabs and click the
   TO:, **CC:**, or **BC:** button on the right side of the view to
   place the names into the personal group list.

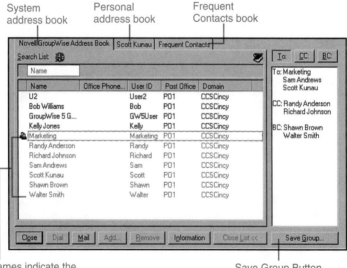

FIGURE 9.2   The Address Book with several names to include in
a personal group.

3. Click the Save Group button in the lower-right corner of
   the screen. The Save As Group dialog box appears as
   shown in Figure 9.3.

4. Name the group. Try to use a name that helps you recognize which users the group represents and pick the address book to save it in and then click OK. You can now use this group to quickly address messages.

5. If you need to modify the members of the group you have created, open the address book, select the personal group, modify each of the fields (TO: CC: BC:) where users appear and then save the group again, using the same name.

Name group here —

Add an optional
comment about the —
personal group

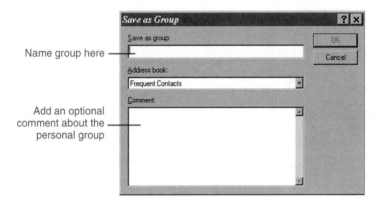

FIGURE 9.3 The Save as Group dialog box.

 Can't Pick and Choose A message that is addressed using a group will be sent to all group members. You cannot select a group and then single out certain users of the group that the message will be sent to.

ADDING A NEW ENTRY INTO YOUR PERSONAL ADDRESS BOOK

GroupWise 5 now gives you a contact manager application right inside the Address Book. You access this application via your personal address book, which typically appears as a tab with your first and last name on it, in the Address Book application. You can add entries to use for addressing messages or for keeping track of clients. You can create as many address book tabs to organize names and addresses as you want. These books can be opened and closed whenever you need to find a contact. Follow these steps to add an entry into your personal address book list.

1. Open the GroupWise 5 Address Book and then click on the tab with your first and last name on it. This tab represents your personal address book by default. If this tab is not showing, choose the Open command from the File menu and then click the book you want to open.

 Too Many/Few Books?   You organize your personal address lists into Address Book "books" that can be opened and closed at anytime. You can create and maintain as many books as you need. However, too many books may make working with the contact manager piece of the Address Book more difficult than it should be because of the need to keep track of which books your contacts appear on.

 Frequent Contact   Whenever you send a message to a user, the GroupWise 5 Address Book application automatically adds that person's name and information to your Frequent Contacts tab, if it is open.

2. Click on the Add button. The New Entry dialog box appears (see Figure 9.4). In the Select the entry type: list, choose to add either a person, resource, or organization. Then click OK.

3. The Information for New Entry dialog box appears (see Figure 9.5). Complete the informational fields and click OK. This will add the person to your address book and make it possible for you to address a message to him (Lesson 4) or use automatic telephone dialing software (see Lesson 16) to call him using one of a variety of phone numbers you can keep within their record.

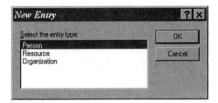

FIGURE 9.4   The New Entry dialog box.

   TIP   **E-mail Type/Greetings**   To properly address a message using your personal address book, be sure to enter an e-mail type such as **Internet** for an Internet address or **NGW** for a GroupWise 5 user address. Add an entry in the **Greetings** field to attach a greeting to each message you send to this user, such as **Dear user**.

Required field

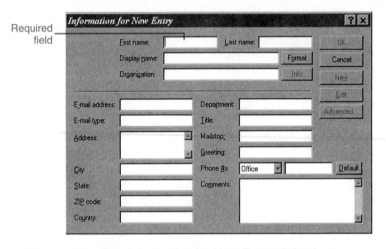

FIGURE 9.5   The Information for New Entry dialog box.

In this lesson you learned how to use the GroupWise 5 Address Book to address messages, how to create a personal group, and finally how to add an entry into your personal address book. In the next lesson you will learn about the GroupWise 5 calendar.

WORKING WITH YOUR CALENDAR

In this lesson you'll learn how to work with your day calendar by placing personal appointments, notes, and tasks onto it. You'll also learn to change to the different calendar views and to print your day calendar.

The scheduling/calendar feature of GroupWise 5 is one of its most powerful features. You can place personal appointments onto your calendar or you can schedule appointments with others. You should add both your personal appointments and appointments scheduled with others to your calendar. Then, when other users search your calendar, via Busy Search (see Lesson 11), for available meeting times, your entire schedule, both personal and business items, will appear on the calendar.

VIEWING YOUR DAY CALENDAR

You can view your calendar either as a view from your mailbox or in a separate window as your day calendar. The view in your mailbox will only show appointments sent to you, whereas the separate day calendar view will show you both appointments you've set and those sent to you from other users. By default, the calendar view in your mailbox only shows appointments but gives you the ability to display tasks and notes. The default day calendar view in a separate window shows all three types of messages (see Lesson 12 for more information on tasks and notes). Follow these steps to view your day calendar:

1. Choose the Windows menu and click on the Calendar View command. This will open the GroupWise 5 Day calendar view (see Figure 10.1). It will show you group and personal appointments as well as all of your tasks and notes.

> **Personal Appointment** An event you have scheduled for yourself only. A mail message does not appear in your mailbox because the personal appointment goes right to your calendar.
>
> **Group Appointment** One of the types of messages you can send is the appointment message. This type of appointment is sent as a regular message. It will appear in your mailbox and be placed onto the calendar view of your mailbox. You will also be able to see it on one of the calendar views.

2. In the calendar on the left side of the Day Calendar view, click on the day of the week you want to display or add personal appointments to. Notice in the three month calendar that some days appear bold. These bolded dates indicate events are scheduled on them.

3. Click on one of the days that is in bold. The events, appointments, tasks, and notes will appear in the appropriate windows on the right side of the Day Calendar view.

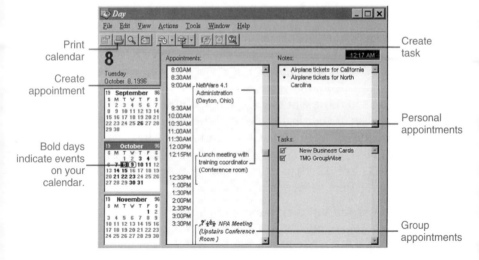

FIGURE 10.1 Day view of your personal calendar.

CHANGE THE CALENDAR VIEWS

GroupWise 5 offers a lot of flexibility in viewing your calendar. Examples include viewing your calendar in the default Day view, as a Desk Calendar or as Week at a glance view. Follow these steps to change your calendar view from the default Day view to one of the others listed in Table 10.1.

TABLE 10.1   CALENDAR VIEWS FOR GROUPWISE 5

THIS VIEW	DOES THIS
Day	Displays Day at a glance
Week	Displays Week at a glance
Year	Displays Year at a glance
Desk Calendar	Displays current day in desk calendar format
Notebook	Displays all of your notes on a given day
Day Projects	Displays day calendar, notes list, project lists, and your mailbox in different windows
Day Planner	Displays four calendar months along with appointments, tasks, and notes
Project Planner	Displays four calendar months along with mailbox folders plus tasks and notes
Appointment (sm)	Displays daily appointments in a small window
Note (sm)	Displays daily notes in a small window
Task (sm)	Displays daily tasks in a small window

1. Choose the Windows menu and click on the Calendar View. Your Day calendar will appear on the screen.

2. Choose the Edit, Change To More command to open the Change To dialog box (see Figure 10.2).

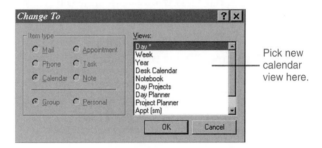

Pick new calendar view here.

FIGURE 10.2   The Change To dialog box showing the different calendar views you can select.

3. Browse through the list in the Views portion of the dialog box and select a calendar view different from the default Day view. Click OK when you have selected the new view. Figure 10.3 displays the desk calendar view.

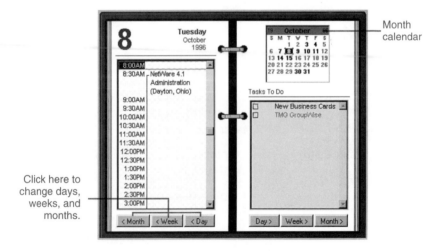

Month calendar

Click here to change days, weeks, and months.

FIGURE 10.3   Your Desk Calendar view.

Depending upon the view you select, you will have a variety of options from which to choose. In the desk calendar view, you can change the day, the month, or the week by clicking on one of the buttons near the bottom of the view. To quickly change to another day, simply click on that day in the one month calendar near the top-right of the desk calendar.

CREATING A PERSONAL APPOINTMENT AND TASK

To keep track of your own personal activities, you can use your GroupWise 5 calendar to create personal appointments, tasks, and notes. It is easy to create or "send" yourself a personal event. No message is sent through the GroupWise 5 system, rather it goes directly to your calendar. To create a personal appointment, task, and note, follow these steps:

1. Choose the Windows menu and click on the Calendar View. Your Day calendar will appear on the screen (see Figure 10.1).

2. Double-click the **Appointments**, **Tasks**, or **Notes** portion of your Day calendar. This will open a personal appointment, task, or note view. Figure 10.4 shows the Personal Appointment view.

3. Type a subject, place, start date (if other than the default date) and time and duration and message for your personal appointment (see Lesson 11 on appointments), task, or note (see Lesson 12 on tasks and notes). Use either the calendar and clock buttons to set the date and time or type them in the date and time fields. Click OK to place the personal appointment, task, or note onto your calendar.

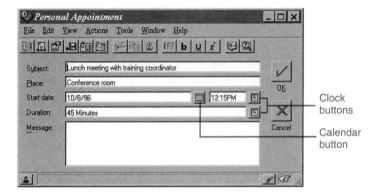

FIGURE 10.4   The Personal Appointment dialog box.

4. The personal item you created should immediately appear on your calendar view on the day you scheduled it.

 **Recurring Appointment?**   You can schedule a recurring personal appointment or task by using the Auto-Date feature. (See Lesson 11 for the Auto-Date feature.)

PRINTING YOUR CALENDAR

GroupWise 5 allows you to print your calendar and possibly use it as a day planner. Appointments, tasks, and notes will print on a predesigned form for a day planner or on blank paper. Follow these steps to print your calendar:

1. Choose the File menu and the Print Calendar command. This will open the Print Calendar dialog box (see Figure 10.5).

2. Click on the Calendar type box to choose either a predesigned form (Figure 10.5 shows Franklin Quest) or plain text. Depending upon your choice in the Calendar type field, you may be able to select from several sizes and styles of paper as well as the page layout.

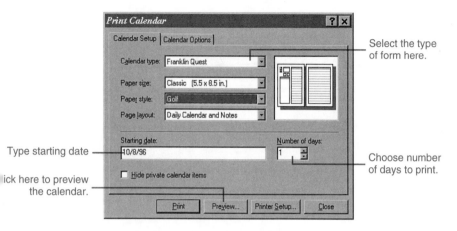

Select the type
of form here.

Type starting date

Choose number
of days to print.

ick here to preview
the calendar.

FIGURE 10.5   The Print Calendar dialog box.

3. Choose the starting date and the number of days you
   want to print. You may want to click on the **Preview**
   button to view what the calendar printout will look like
   (see Figure 10.6).

4. Click the Calendar Options tab to select printing options
   regarding text overflow on a given item, the contents of
   the printout, and any necessary adjustment to accommo-
   date preprinted calendar forms. Click Print.

Printer Loaded and Ready?   If you are using a predesigned form, be sure to place the form into your printer,
either as a manual feed document or into the paper tray.

View the next page   Print the calendar

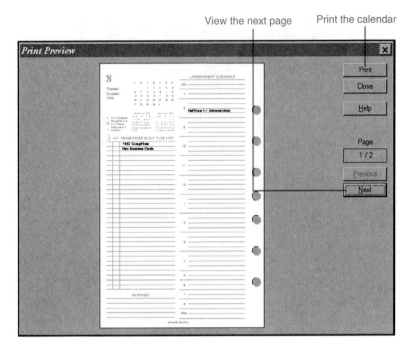

FIGURE 10.6   The Print Preview screen.

In this lesson you learned how to work with your calendar, how to place personal appointments, tasks, and notes on it, and finally how to print your calendar. In the next lesson you will learn how to send an appointment to a group.

SCHEDULING AND RESPONDING TO APPOINTMENTS

In this lesson you'll learn how to send an appointment message, how to use the Auto-Date feature, how to use Busy Search, and finally how to read and accept or decline an appointment.

SCHEDULING APPOINTMENTS

One of the most powerful features of GroupWise 5 is its scheduling functions. You can maintain a calendar with appointments, tasks, and notes on it, look at other user's calendars, search other user's calendars when creating an appointment, and send multiple occurrences of the same appointment using the Auto-Date feature.

However, for scheduling to work in your company or work group, *everyone* must participate and use the scheduling features. If even one person doesn't use the scheduling features completely, the task of scheduling meetings with the Busy Search feature breaks down. If your company has not implemented the scheduling features of GroupWise 5 yet, you can still use it yourself to schedule your own meetings, tasks, and notes (see Lesson 10 for more about working with your calendar).

When you decide to schedule an appointment with others you must:

- Address the appointment message to all recipients, including yourself.

- Provide the dates and times for the appointment. If it's a recurring appointment, set the dates and times for each occurrence.

- Provide a brief description of what the appointment is about.

- Ensure that all recipients are free to attend the appointment by checking their calendars for other commitments.

CREATING THE APPOINTMENT MESSAGE

To schedule a meeting with another user or group of users, use the following steps.

1. Open a new appointment message by choosing the File menu and the New command. Click on the Appointment command to open the Appointment To: dialog box (see Figure 11.1).

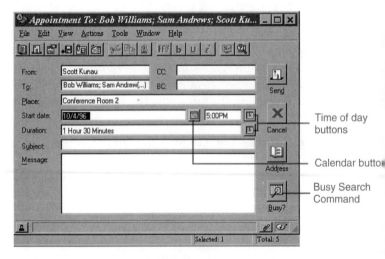

FIGURE 11.1   A new appointment message.

2. Click on the Address button and address the appointment message (see Lesson 9 for more about addresses). When you are done choosing the users from the address book, click OK to return to the Appointment To: dialog box.

3. Choose the calendar button, located at the right of the Start Date: box. The Set Date dialog box appears (see Figure 11.2), which allows you to pick an individual date for the appointment. Click on the date when the appointment is to be scheduled. If your appointment occurs next month or next year, click on the single arrow to move forward or back one month or click on the double arrow to move forward or back one year. If this is a recurring appointment, choose the **Auto-Date** feature (skip to the next task to learn how to use Auto-Date). Choose the date of the appointment and click OK.

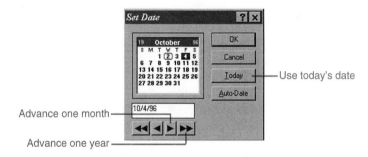

FIGURE 11.2   The Set Date dialog box.

4. Set the beginning time and add the duration of the appointment by clicking on the time of day buttons (see Figure 11.1). This will open the Time Input dialog box. Select the left side of the scale for the start time and the right side of the scale for the stop time. The duration of the appointment will automatically appear in the dialog box. Click OK to return to the appointment message.

5. Confirm that all recipients can attend the appointment by using the Busy Search feature. The Busy Search feature is covered later in this lesson.

6. Type a subject line for the message in the Subject text box. You may also want to type a location in the Place text box so recipients will know where the appointment will be held.

7. Type a brief message. The message should explain the nature of the appointment.

8. Click Send to send the appointment.

Recurring Appointment   An appointment message that appears on multiple dates of a user's calendar. For example, a staff meeting each Wednesday should be sent as a recurring appointment rather than creating individual appointments. Use the Auto-Date feature to set up an appointment that occurs several times.

Schedule a Room?   If your system administrator has created GroupWise 5 resources for things that are checked out or scheduled such as meeting rooms or audio-visual equipment, you can schedule the resources by selecting them from the address book. Resources are maintained by users so when a resource is scheduled an additional message is sent to the owner who can decide to allow its use. This accept or decline operation can be made automatic with rules (see Lesson 20 on rules).

SETTING UP RECURRING APPOINTMENTS

To use the Auto-Date feature to create a recurring appointment, follow these steps.

1. In the Set Date dialog box (see Figure 11.2), click on the Auto-Date button. The Auto-Date dialog box appears as shown in Figure 11.3.

By example tab By formula tab   Advance years

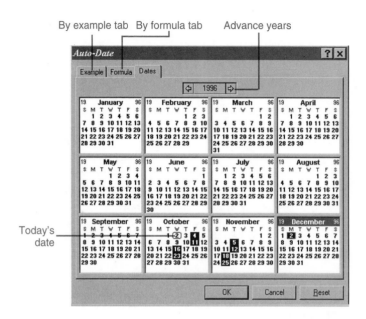

Today's date

FIGURE 11.3   The Auto-Date dialog box using the Dates tab.

2. Set multiple days for the recurring appointment. You have the option to select recurring days by:

Example   Using by Example allows you to schedule the Auto-Date appointment without knowing the exact day of the month. You know meetings are held on the second Wednesday and fourth Friday of each month, for example, so select the month(s) and then the days for the meetings.

Formula   You can use functions and operators to create an Auto-Date formula. This method is provided for those users who prefer to create Auto-Date appointments using formulas. For example, the formula (Wed(2), Wed(3), Wed(4), Fri(5))(Nov) will set up an appointment on the second, third, and fourth Wednesdays along with the fifth Friday in the month of November.

Dates   Select the days you want to include in the appointment from a year at a glance calendar. This method is especially easy when choosing consecutive days for an event, such as a computer class.

3. Figure 11.3 shows Auto-Date by days. When you set the dates, click OK to return to the Appointment To: dialog box (see Figure 11.1).

 Separate Messages   Each date you choose for a recurring appointment causes a separate appointment message to be sent. The GroupWise 5 system does this so users can accept or decline an individual day's recurring appointment.

USING BUSY SEARCH

If all users in your workgroup or company utilize GroupWise 5's calendar features, Busy Search will become a powerful tool. After addressing your message and picking the date and times the appointment will likely occur, follow these steps:

1. In the Appointment To: dialog box, click on the Busy Search button in the appointment view. The Choose Appointment Time dialog box appears (see Figure 11.4).

 No Busy Search?   You must address the appointment message to users before the Busy Search will function properly. Do not select the Busy? button until you have completed the addressing portion of the appointment (see the previous task).

2. Click on the Available Times tab to see if all users are available. Users are available if you do not see any shading on the busy search screen during the proposed appointment time.

3. If users' schedules are busy, click the **Individual Schedules** tab and browse through the user's schedule and see when an opening for all users is possible.

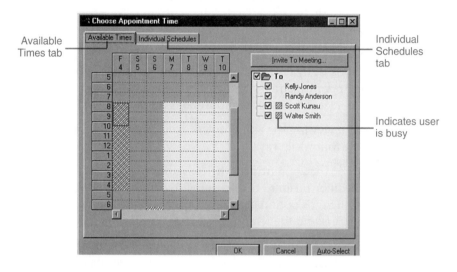

FIGURE 11.4   The Choose Appointment Time dialog box.

4. After you have found free time in everyone's schedule, make the necessary adjustments in the appointment time you have created and then click OK.

 Finding Free Time Fast   An easy way to find adequate free time in everyone's schedule is to use the Auto-Select feature from the Busy Search dialog box. This allows Busy Search to find the first available time all recipients have free. If the first Auto-Select time is not acceptable, click the Auto-Select button again to search for the next available time.

RESPONDING TO APPOINTMENTS

When an appointment arrives in your mailbox, you will have the opportunity to accept or decline it and offer a comment or reason, if necessary, for acting on the appointment. To accept or decline an appointment, follow these steps.

1. Open the new appointment by double-clicking it in your mailbox or by double-clicking it from your calendar view. The Appointment From: dialog box appears (see Figure 11.5). (See Lesson 10 for more about the calendar view.)

2. After reviewing the appointment, you can respond in any of the following ways:

   Accept the appointment. If you accept the appointment, you will be taken to the Accept with comment dialog box. Although it's optional, adding a comment helps the sender to understand the reason for your response.

   Decline the appointment. If you decline the appointment, you will be taken to the Decline with comment dialog box. Although it's optional, adding a comment helps the sender to understand the reason for your response. If you decline, the appointment is removed from your calendar and mailbox folder.

   Close the appointment message without taking action on it.

   Delegate the appointment. To delegate a message, click on the Delegate icon in the Toolbar or choose **Actions** and choose **Delegate**.

 Delegate   To assign the meeting to another GroupWise 5 user. If you can't attend the meeting you can delegate a staff member to go in your place. The appointment message would then be sent along to that delegate user.

Accept Decline

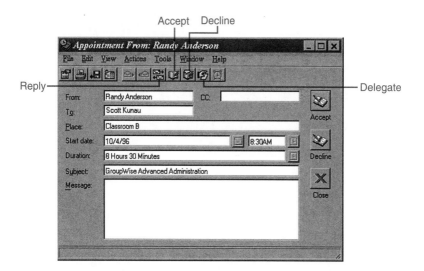

Reply ————

Delegate

FIGURE 11.5   A new appointment waiting to be accepted or declined.

 All Instances?   If this appointment is a recurring one, you will be prompted to accept, decline, or delegate all instances or just this instance of the appointment.

In this lesson you learned how to set the date and time of an appointment, how to use the Auto-Date and Busy Search features and how to accept or decline an appointment. In the next lesson you will learn how to send and receive tasks and notes.

12

SENDING AND RECEIVING TASKS AND NOTES

In this lesson you will learn how to create, send, receive, and take action on tasks and notes and how to view both of these features on your calendar.

WHAT ARE TASKS AND NOTES?

Tasks and notes are two additional types of messages you can send with GroupWise 5. While either will appear on your calendar as reminders, tasks will appear each day on your calendar until you mark them completed and, by default, will appear only on the day it was sent.

You can prioritize tasks on the Tasks portion of your calendar when you send a task to others or when you create a personal task. Assigning a task priority only helps to organize tasks together on the task list of your calendar; it doesn't help you get it done any quicker nor will the priority of one task change upon completion of another.

 Priorities The task priority affects how a task appears in the task list of your calendar, such as A1, B2, and so on and is set in the Priority field of the task to: view. The sending priority affects how the task message actually moves through the GroupWise 5 system. You set sending priority with Send Options located in the Properties dialog box under the File menu of the task window.

CREATING AND SENDING A TASK

Follow these steps to create and send a task to other users:

1. In your GroupWise 5 mailbox screen choose File, New from the menu. Select Task. (You can also click on the New Task icon in the toolbar.) The Task To: dialog box appears as shown in Figure 12.1.

> **TIP**   **Personal Tasks**   If you are creating a personal task for your own calendar, open the Calendar View under the Window menu, double-click on the task area and fill in the Personal Task message view. (See Lesson 10 for more information on working with your calendar).

2. To choose the recipients for this task, click on the Address button to access the Address Book. When you have completed choosing the recipients, click OK in the Address Book to return to the Task To: dialog box.

> **TIP**   **Forget Yourself?**   If you are part of the team to complete the task, don't forget to include your own userID when addressing the task. You can type your userID in the TO:, CC:, or BC: fields or choose yourself from the Address Book at the same time you choose other recipients.

3. Choose the start and due dates by first clicking on the respective calendar buttons near the date fields to access the Set Date dialog box. The Set Date dialog box appears, as shown in Figure 12.2, with the current date highlighted. Click on the date you want to start the task and click OK, then repeat this step to choose the due date. You can also type the start and due dates in both fields.

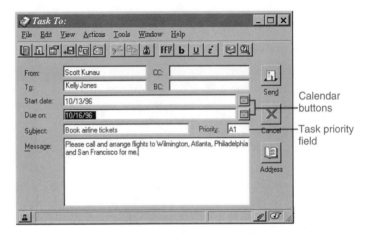

FIGURE 12.1 A new task ready to send.

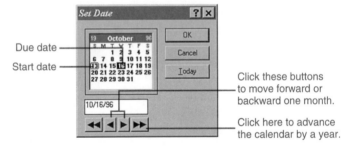

FIGURE 12.2 The Set Date dialog box showing start and due dates for a task.

4. Type a subject.

5. **(Optional)** Set a task priority (A1, A2, 1, or C3 for example) to group your tasks together. You should type a message describing the task. You can also attach files to the task, by clicking on the **Attachments** button (see Lesson 5 for more about attachments).

6. Click Send when you have completed all the information.

Taking Action on a Task

Tasks, like appointments and notes, must have some sort of action taken on them. A task will appear in your GroupWise 5 mailbox represented by an icon that looks like a pile of papers with check marks (see Lesson 1). It will also appear on your calendar, like a note or an appointment. If you open a task to take action, the icon appears as though a piece of paper is being torn off. Follow these steps to take action on a task:

1. Find a task in your mailbox and double-click it. You can also right-click on the task and choose **Open** from the Quick Menu.

2. You have three options: Accept, Decline, or Close the task view:

   • **Accept** If you choose to accept the task by clicking on the **Accept** button, the Accept with Comment dialog will appear (see Figure 12.3) and the task will be placed on the task list on your calendar.

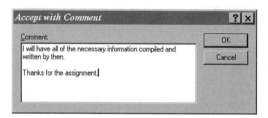

Figure 12.3   The Accept with Comment dialog box for a task.

   • **Decline** If you choose to decline the task by clicking on the **Decline** button, the Decline with Comment dialog box will appear (see Figure 12.4). If you decline a task, it will be removed from both your mailbox and your task list.

   • **Close** Closes the task dialog box and returns you back to your mailbox.

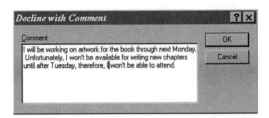

FIGURE 12.4   The Decline with Comment dialog box for a task.

Task Status   If you accept or decline a task and offer the optional comment explaining your action, a status message will be sent back to the sender of the task to update them.

COMPLETING A TASK

Once you have accepted a task, you will obviously need to complete it. Once a task has been completed there are a few ways to mark it as complete:

- Open the task from one of your mailbox folders or from the task list in one of your calendar views (see Lesson 10 "Working with Your Calendar"). Click in the Completed box in the lower-right corner of the task From: view.

- If you don't want to open the task From: view to mark the task completed, select the task and then choose Actions, Mark Completed.

- Click your mouse in the small box that will appear to the left of the task on your task list from one of your calendar views. A red check will appear, marking the task complete.

In all cases, when you mark a task complete, a status message will be sent to the original sender to update them. If you make a mistake and mark completed a task that is not completed, simply remove the red check mark from the box on your task list.

CREATING A NOTE

GroupWise 5 offers you the ability to inform users, via a note message, about a particular event. A note might be considered similar to a bulletin board posting. Follow these steps to create a note to other users.

1. In your GroupWise 5 mailbox screen choose the File menu and the New command. Select Note. The Note To: dialog box appears as shown in Figure 12.5.

Personal Note If you are creating a personal note for your own calendar, open the Calendar View under the Window menu, double-click on the note area and fill in the Personal Note message view.

2. Click the Address button to access the Address Book and choose the recipients of this note. When you have completed choosing the recipients, click OK in the Address Book to return to the Note To: dialog box.

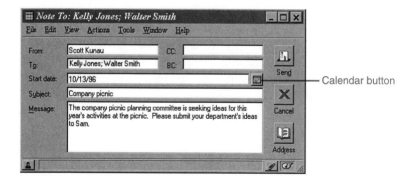

FIGURE 12.5   A new note ready to send.

3. Choose the date or dates that you want the note to appear on recipients' calendars. To choose the date, click the calendar button located to the right of the start date text

box. The Set Date dialog box appears with the current date highlighted. Click the single date or click the Auto-Date button to select multiple dates for the note (see Lesson 11 for more on the calendar and the AutoDate feature). Remember, you can also click in the Start date: text box and type the single date for the note.

4. Type the subject.

5. **(Optional)** Type a message and add an attachment to the note.

6. Click Send when you have completed the note.

TAKING ACTION ON A NOTE

Like a task, you need to take action on a note that you receive. You can accept it, decline it, or close it without taking action. If you accept or decline, the Accept with Comment or the Decline with Comment dialog box will appear on your screen (see Figures 12.3 and 12.4). You can optionally type a comment and then click **OK**.

In general, when you receive a task or note from another user, you will see it appear in your GroupWise 5 mailbox and on your calendar. Figure 12.6 displays the Day Calendar view (see Lesson 10) showing accepted, completed, and new tasks and notes as well as an appointment (see Lesson 11 for more about appointments).

Personal appointment

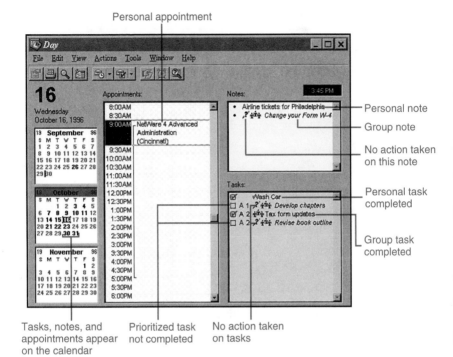

Personal note
Group note
No action taken on this note
Personal task completed
Group task completed

Tasks, notes, and appointments appear on the calendar

Prioritized task not completed

No action taken on tasks

FIGURE 12.6 The Day Calendar showing tasks, notes, and an appointment.

In this lesson you learned how to create, send, and take action on tasks and notes. In the next lesson you will learn how to manage your documents using GroupWise 5 libraries.

13 LESSON

MANAGING DOCUMENTS WITH LIBRARIES

In this lesson you'll learn how to create a document in a Library, how to share a document with other users, how to import documents into a Library, and how to check documents in and out of a Library.

UNDERSTANDING GROUPWISE 5 DOCUMENT LIBRARY FEATURES

GroupWise 5 document management is new and exciting technology that allows users to create and store documents, (spreadsheets and letters for example) and make reference to them from their mailbox. The document management system incorporated into GroupWise 5 is part of the Soft Solutions file management technology that has been available for several years.

When you create a document within GroupWise 5, you add that document to a selected Library. Several new applications, like WordPerfect 7, Word, and Excel 7 offer GroupWise 5 Document Management integration. You are given the option to save documents created in integrated applications into Libraries whenever you choose Save or Save As. When you choose Open from an integrated application, you have the option to open a document from within a library or by using the standard File, Open method (see Figure 13.1).

Once a document has been created or imported into a Library, it can only be accessed from GroupWise 5 because it is compressed into the Library database and encrypted for security purposes. The author of a document controls access to it through sharing. Other users can be granted access to view, edit, delete, and modify the properties of a chosen document.

Choose document here.

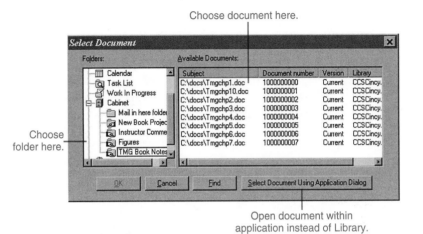

Choose folder here.

Open document within application instead of Library.

FIGURE 13.1   Opening a document with an integrated application.

Library   A collection of documents and document properties stored in databases and directories in the GroupWise 5 system.

Are You on the List?   In order to use the Library and document management features of GroupWise 5, your system administrator must configure a Library and add you to the user list.

CREATING AND STORING A DOCUMENT IN THE LIBRARY

Follow these steps to create a document and place it into a GroupWise 5 Library.

1. Select the folder in your mailbox where the document icon/reference will be placed.

2. Choose the File menu, select the New command and then choose Document. The New Document dialog box appears (see Figure 13.2).

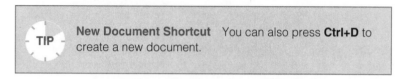

New Document Shortcut You can also press **Ctrl+D** to create a new document.

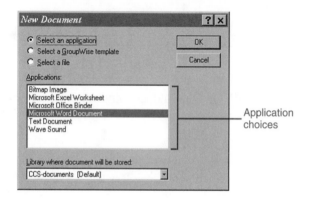

FIGURE **13.2**   The New Document dialog box.

3. If any integrated applications are available (WordPerfect, Word, Excel), choose the software program, or choose a file you want to use as a template to create the new document or choose the GroupWise 5 template you will be using to create the document. Click OK.

4. In the New Document dialog box, type subject information for the new document. The subject information you type will appear in the subject column in your GroupWise 5 mailbox. Click OK to create the document icon.

Open Application Now You can elect to open the application and work on the document at the same time it is created in a GroupWise 5 Library. Click the Open this document now check box before clicking OK to create the document.

IMPORTING EXISTING DOCUMENTS INTO A LIBRARY

You already have a number of documents stored either on the network or on your local hard drive and you want to place these documents into a GroupWise 5 Library. You can import your documents into a Library, providing easy access to them from within GroupWise 5. Importing documents not only facilitates your access but allows you to share the documents with other GroupWise 5 users. Follow these steps to import documents into a Library.

1. From your mailbox, choose the File Menu, Import Documents command. The Select Files to Import dialog box appears (see Figure 13.3).

2. Choose the Add Files button to add documents to the Files to import list. Be sure that the **Quick import** check box is selected. Click Next>.

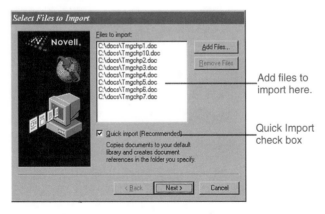

FIGURE 13.3   The Select Files to Import dialog box.

Quick Import   Use the Quick Import process to quickly import documents into a GroupWise 5 Library, assign a default subject, and create a document reference icon in a mailbox folder of your choice.

3. Choose the mailbox folder where document reference icons will be created. You are not required to create a document reference icon, but doing so will make accessing documents much easier. Click Next and then click Finish. A status bar appears showing you the import progress. When the import process is complete, document references appear in the selected folder (see Figure 13.4).

Selected folder   Subject column displays   Document references
                         subject information   in the selected folder

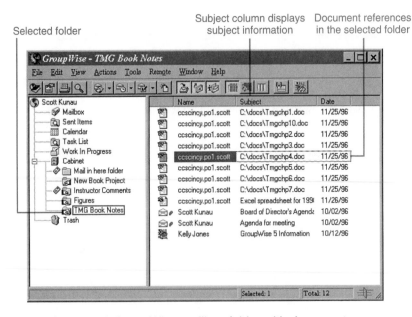

FIGURE 13.4   A GroupWise mailbox folder with document references.

VIEWING AND MODIFYING DOCUMENT PROPERTIES

At this point you can open the document properties to view and modify some of those properties. Properties are necessary for saving, retrieving, and searching for documents. You can view and change document properties from the Properties dialog box. Properties are organized into several tabbed pages:

- **Document** Displays information about the document, including the Library it was placed in, its document number, the subject, author, document type, and creation information.

- **Version** Displays version information, including creation date, modification date, and file extension.

- **Sharing** Displays sharing information for a document. The author/creator of the document reference can assign additional access to the document, decide to share it, and modify existing share access.

- **Activity Log** Displays the activity that has occurred on the selected document.

Follow these steps to access the document properties.

1. Right-click to select a document in your mailbox folder and open the Quick Menu. Choose the Properties command. This will cause the Properties dialog box to appear on your screen.

2. **(Optional)** To view information about the creator of the document and the document type, click the **Document** tab (see Figure 13.5). To view information about the current version of a document, click the **Version** tab. Usually, you shouldn't attempt to change information on these.

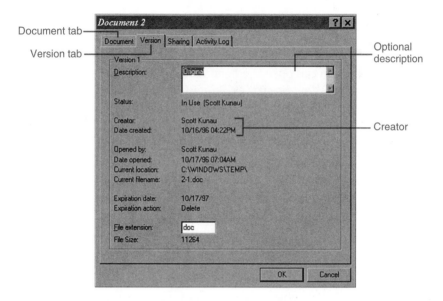

FIGURE 13.5   The Document properties dialog box.

3. To share a document, click on the Sharing tab (see Figure 13.6).

> **Sharing** Giving access rights to other users to view, modify, or delete documents you have created or imported into a GroupWise 5 Library. The Sharing tab provides you the opportunity to Not Share, Share with specific groups or users, and Set version-level security with selected groups of users.

4. Click the Shared with button and type a user's name into the Name field and click the Add User button. The user name is displayed in the Share list. (You can also click on the Address Book icon to browse and pick users out of the Address Book.)

5. In the Share list box, highlight each user name and select the various access rights the highlighted user will possess on this particular document. Click OK when you are finished.

6. **(Optional)** Click on the **Version Level Security** button if you want to specifically control a user's access to versions of the document. You can choose to give access to the Official version, the Current version, and Other versions of the document. Once you complete choosing specific access to the document, click OK to return to the Sharing tab. Click OK to return to your mailbox.

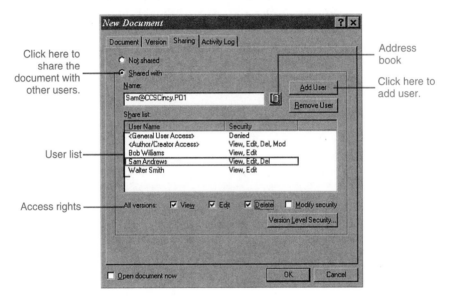

FIGURE 13.6   The Sharing Tab of the New Document dialog box.

ACCESSING A DOCUMENT

Once a document has been created and shared, users can access it by opening the shared folder where a document reference to it exists and then double-clicking on the reference to open the document. The user who is trying to access the document must have Edit rights to actually open the document, otherwise, it will only be accessible via the QuickViewer (under the View menu). If the document is accessed by an authorized user, GroupWise 5 sets an *In Use* status on the document to prevent other users from editing it while you have it open. After you close the document, GroupWise 5 will remove the *In Use* status, which will allow another user to access the document.

If you require lengthy access to a version of the document for multiple editing sessions, you can check the document out of the Library. This prevents other users from editing the document but may allow them to view it with the QuickViewer if they have view access. Meanwhile, the document you check out is copied to check-out location you specify and remains locked until you check it back into the Library. Follow these steps to check out a document from a Library.

1. Select the document you want to check-out. Choose the Actions menu and the Check-Out command. This will cause the Check-Out dialog box to appear (see Figure 13.7).

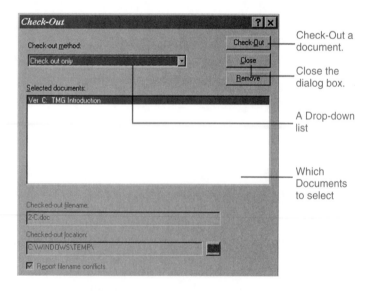

FIGURE 13.7   The Check-Out document dialog box.

Check-Out When you want to lock the document you are working on for extended periods of time. For example, you can use Check-Out to lock documents you want to work on when you are at home or away from the office. Users with View access to the document will be able to view it but not make modifications until you check it back into the Library.

2. In the Check-Out dialog box, choose the Check-out method, either to check-out and copy the document or to simply check-out the document. If you choose to check-out and copy the document, you will need to provide a filename and location, or accept the default filename and default location listed in Checked-out filename and Checked-out location. By default you will be warned about filename conflicts in the Checked-out location. When you have chosen the Check-out method and other items, click the Check-Out button and then choose Close.

3. Access the application you created the document with and open it. Make your modifications, and save and close the document in the application.

CHECKING THE DOCUMENT INTO THE LIBRARY

Once you have completed work on the document, you will need to check the document back in to the Library. You have the option to check-in the document and move it from the temporary location it was stored on your local hard drive (thus deleting it from this location) or check-in and copy the document, which leaves a copy in your checked-out location. You can also simply check-in the document, which will not update the document with your changes. If you require additional time on the document, but want others to see updated versions of the document, you can update the document without checking it in to the Library.

When you check the document back in to the Library, you can specify which version will be placed back in to the Library: the checked-out version, which updates the version you checked-out originally; New version, that creates a new version of the document; or New Document, which creates a new document and document reference with specific properties and user access (see information earlier in this task for specifics). Follow these steps to check the document back in to the Library.

1. Return to GroupWise 5 and highlight the checked-out document in the mailbox folder where the document reference is located.

2. Choose the Actions menu and the Check-In command. This will cause the Check-In dialog box to appear on your screen (see Figure 13.8).

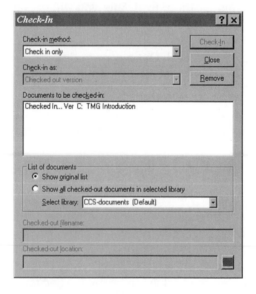

FIGURE 13.8 The Check-In dialog box.

3. Click on the Check-in method drop-down list box and choose one of the check-in methods. You can move the document back into the Library, place a copy of it into the Library, check it in only, or update it without checking it in.

Location and Filename Required If you check-in and move the document, you will be required to input the checked-out filename and location of the check-out document before you can check the document into the Library.

In this lesson you learned how to create a document and how to place it into a GroupWise 5 Library. You also learned how to import documents into a Library, how to view and modify properties of document references, how to check-out a document, and how to check it back in to a Library. In the next lesson, you will learn how to create and use shared folders.

CREATING AND USING SHARED FOLDERS

In this lesson you'll learn how to share personal folders with others and how to install shared folders into your GroupWise 5 Cabinet after someone has shared a folder with you.

Work flow and sharing information are a big part of GroupWise 5. You can easily share parts of your mailbox with others by first creating private folders in your Cabinet (see Lesson 8 for more about creating folders) and then sharing them. Folders can be shared with individual users or with a group. Once a folder is shared with another user, you use it to store discussion messages (see Lesson 15) as well as any other type of message (mail message, task, note, phone message, document) you want the other users to see.

SET UP A SHARED FOLDER

When you let others share a folder, you determine their access rights. Each user can have different access rights. For example, you may want to let certain users read, modify, or delete items in a folder, while other users can only read the items in the folder.

To set up a shared folder, follow these steps. Be sure to review Lesson 8 on creating a folder in your Cabinet.

1. Highlight a folder in your Cabinet that you want to share. Right-click on this folder and choose the Sharing command from the Quickmenu. The Figures Properties dialog box appears (see Figure 14.1). (You can also choose the **Properties** command from the Quickmenu and then choose the **Sharing** tab in the Properties dialog box.)

2. On the Sharing tab, select the Shared with option.

3. Click on the address book button to open the Address Book and select the names of users who will share the folder. You can also type the names of users into the Name box and then click on the **Add User** button.

 Type Usernames? If you type the names of users into the Name box, be sure to select the **Add User** button to move the user into the Share list box.

4. To set additional access options, select a user in the Share list, then click each access option in the Additional access portion of the dialog box to grant specific access to the user. Remember each user in the Share list can have different access rights to the shared folder. Click OK when you are done selecting access options. The Shared Folder Notification dialog box appears so you can prepare to notify users they have been granted access rights to one of your mailbox folders. (See the next task on notifying these users about the shared folder.)

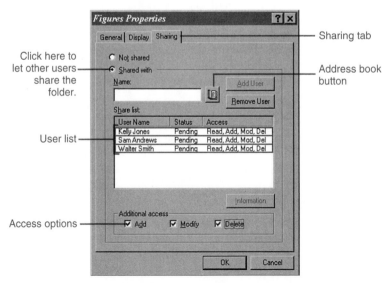

FIGURE 14.1 Shared folder properties showing users and access options selected.

NOTIFYING OTHERS OF THE SHARED FOLDER

Once you set up and grant access to the shared folder, GroupWise 5 will need to notify each user about the shared folder. When you click **OK** from the Figures Properties/Sharing tab screen, the Shared Folder Notification dialog box will appear. Follow these steps to notify users about the new shared folder.

1. Confirm the participants who will share the folder.

2. Use the default subject or type a subject of your own in the Subject box.

3. Type an optional message informing users of the shared folder and click OK. A message indicating the user has access to the new shared folder will be sent to each participant.

INSTALLING A SHARED FOLDER

You just received a message regarding a new shared folder. Follow these steps to set up your mailbox so you may access the new shared folder.

1. Double-click on the Shared Folder notification message to open it and the Install Shared Folder dialog box will appear (see Figure 14.2). Click the Next > button.

2. In the second dialog box pick the location (folder) in your mailbox where you want to install the new shared folder (see Figure 14.3). You can see the full list of locations (folders) by clicking one or more times on the **Down** and **Left** buttons to scroll through a list of your own mailbox folders. Notice that as you click the down or left buttons, each folder will appear highlighted as you move through the list.

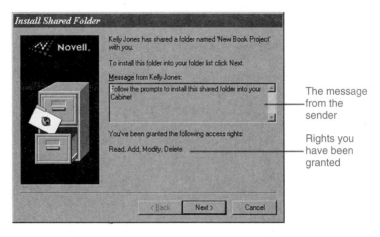

The message
from the
sender

Rights you
have been
granted

FIGURE 14.2   The Install Shared Folder dialog box.

Select the Folder If you know which mailbox folder the new shared folder will be installed into, directly select that folder with your mouse, rather than scrolling through the folder list.

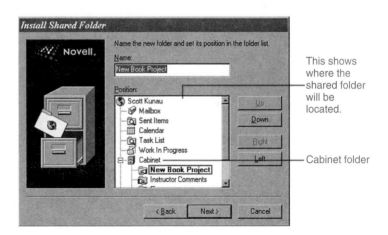

This shows
where the
shared folder
will be
located.

Cabinet folder

FIGURE 14.3   Choosing the location of the new shared folder.

3. Click Next > to proceed to the dialog box where you can optionally add a description for the new shared folder.

4. Click Finish to complete the shared folder installation in your mailbox.

You can begin placing messages and documents into the new shared folder, provided you have the access rights to create new items in the folder. If you are set-up to only read items in the folder, open the folder and double-click on a message or document to read it. Figure 14.4 shows you how the folders you share with others will look and how folders that other users have shared with you will look in your Cabinet.

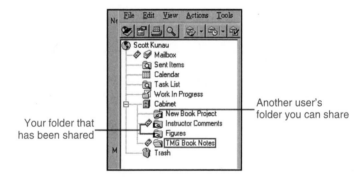

Your folder that has been shared

Another user's folder you can share

FIGURE 14.4   The Mailbox view showing shared folders.

In this lesson you learned how to share a personal folder and how to install a folder that someone else has shared with you into your Cabinet folder. In the next lesson you will learn how to create discussion items in the shared folder.

STARTING AND USING DISCUSSIONS

15

In this lesson you'll learn how to start a discussion thread and how to reply or participate in a discussion carried on within the GroupWise 5 system.

One of the major benefits of groupware technology is the capability to share thoughts in the form of discussion messages. GroupWise 5 provides the capability to start and carry on conversations or discussions and makes it possible to "thread" them together. Users can reply back to the original post that started the discussion or to any reply posted by any user.

 Shared Folders? Discussions can only be carried on within shared folders. See Lesson 14 to learn more about sharing folders.

STARTING A DISCUSSION

Follow these steps to start a discussion message thread in one of your shared folders.

1. Open one of your shared folders by clicking it once. If any messages or discussions are already in the folder, they will appear.

2. Choose the File menu and the New command, then select Discussion. This will cause the New Discussion dialog box to appear on your screen (see Figure 15.1).

3. Type the subject that the discussion will be about and press the Tab key to move into the Message box.

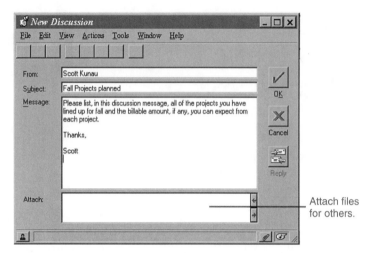

FIGURE 15.1   The New Discussion dialog box.

How to Address?   You do not address this type of message to a particular user. All users who have been granted access rights to read items in the shared folder will be able to see discussion items, participate in discussions, and offer replies. (See Lesson 14 on granting access rights to shared folders.)

Do You Want This Discussed?   Any item, mail message, document, and so on, that is placed into a shared folder automatically is available to be a discussion item. This is actually a benefit because it allows you to drag messages to shared folders to start discussions.

4. Type a message that begins the discussion.

5. **(Optional)** You can attach files to discussions to allow all of the participating users to access the files attached. (See Lesson 5 for more about attaching files.)

6. Click OK to post the message into the shared folder and begin the discussion.

 Post   To mail or place a message into a shared folder. This is similar to posting a message to an online forum or Internet newsgroup because it enables users to reply to your message both publicly and privately.

READING AND REPLYING TO A DISCUSSION

Once a user has posted a message into a shared folder, a discussion can begin about the topic. It is good "discussion etiquette" to avoid straying too far from the posted topic. If your comments differ from the posted discussion topic, and you have the access rights to create new items (discussions) in the shared folder, consider starting another discussion. Follow these steps to reply to and follow a discussion thread.

1. Open the shared folder where the discussion thread is posted.

2. Double-click on the discussion you want to read or participate in. This will open the discussion post.

3. Read the post and click Reply to open a discussion reply. This will cause the Reply dialog box to appear on your screen (see Figure 15.2).

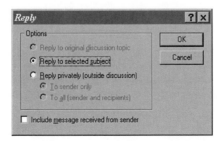

FIGURE 15.2   The Reply dialog box showing reply options.

4. Choose the type of reply you will offer: **Reply to selected subject**, or **Reply privately (outside discussion)**. If you choose the latter, you are given the option
to reply to just the sender (originator of the discussion) or
to all who have participated in the discussion.

5. Click OK to close the Reply dialog box and open a message screen where you will type the reply message. When
you are done writing your reply, click OK to post your
reply.

VIEWING DISCUSSIONS AS THREADS IN SHARED FOLDERS

In order to properly view a discussion thread, you must first open
the shared folder in which it appears. Next click on the toolbar
icon to view the folder as a discussion thread. The original post in
the discussion will appear as an icon with a pin holding the notice on a bulletin board. Each subsequent post will appear indented slightly under the particular post it connects to (see Figure
15.3).

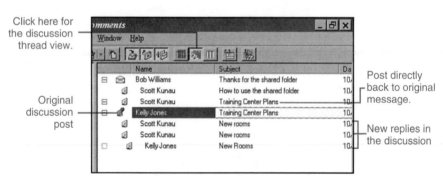

FIGURE 15.3   Mailbox showing a shared folder with a discussion
thread.

In Figure 15.3 Kelly Jones starts a discussion about "Training Center Plans." Scott Kunau offers two posts entitled "New Rooms." Kelly responds back to the "New Rooms" post while Scott adds his thoughts to the original "Training Center Plans" discussion.

In this lesson you have learned how to start a discussion thread, how to reply or participate in a discussion, and how to view and understand a discussion thread. In the next lesson you will learn how to manage your telephone with the Conversation Place application.

16

MANAGING YOUR TELEPHONE WITH CONVERSATION PLACE

In this lesson you'll learn how to use the GroupWise 5 Conversation Place to manage your telephone. You'll also learn about the hardware requirements you will need to make Conversation Place work for you.

The Conversation Place is a new tool that comes with GroupWise 5. Conversation Place is tightly integrated with the GroupWise 5 Address Book (see Lesson 9) and allows you to store phone numbers in the Public Address Book, your Frequent Contacts and Personal Address book and to place calls using those phone numbers. Providing you have the required hardware in place, you can use the Conversation Place to place calls, answer your phone, transfer calls, set up conference calls, and hang up your phone. In order to effectively use Conversation Place, your system administrator will need to provide you with the following hardware and software.

TABLE 16.1 HARDWARE AND SOFTWARE FOR CONVERSATION PLACE

DEVICE	DESCRIPTION
Computer modem	Connects your computer to a telephone line and the TAPI provider.
TAPI provider	Telephone application programming interface device.

DEVICE	DESCRIPTION
TAPI32.DLL	File on your computer that works together with the TAPI provider or TSAPI TServer.
TSAPI TServer	Telephony Server application programming interface device.
CSTA32.DLL	File on your computer that works with the TSAPI hardware.
Client32™	Novell™ Client32™ software on each computer that uses Conversation Place.

Telephony   The technology of integrating computers and telephones.

To use Conversation Place, follow these steps:

1. Choose Tools, Conversation Place from the menu. This will start Conversation Place. The Conversation Place application window appears (see Figure 16.1), an icon appears on the Windows task bar and will continually run in the background, waiting for incoming calls.

Close Conversation Place   Conversation Place application does not stop operating when you close its application window. If you want to stop it from functioning, right-click the Conversation Place icon in the task bar and choose Exit.

TIP **Locations** You should create a Location setup for Conversation Place to use when dialing. Doing so will prevent you from needing to include special line access characters (9 for example) each time you make a call. See the task below to access the Locations dialog box to configure a Location.

 TIP **Starting Conversation Place** You can also start Conversation Place as a separate application from the Windows 95 desktop. Choose the Start menu, Programs, GroupWise 5, and Conversation Place.

FIGURE 16.1 The Conversation Place main screen.

2. To call someone, position your cursor in the Enter Name field and start typing the caller's name. Or, click the address book button and choose the user's name from the public or personal address book tabs or the Frequent Contacts tab in the Address Book and click OK (see Figure 16.2).

Phone Numbers and the Address Book In order to use the Address Book with Conversation Place, the phone numbers of the users you plan to call need to be in either your personal or the public address book. You can add phone number information to the personal address book or your Frequent Contacts book. Your system administrator needs to add the phone numbers to the public address book. You can also type the user's phone number in the Enter Phone Number field each time you make a call.

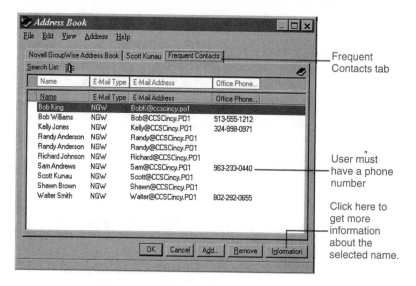

Frequent Contacts tab

User must have a phone number

Click here to get more information about the selected name.

FIGURE 16.2   The Address Book showing phone numbers.

3. Make sure the user's phone number appears in the Phone Number field of the Conversation Place application window and click Dial.

4. When the phone starts ringing, pick up the receiver.

TIP   **Recent Calls** You can quickly dial one of the ten most recent incoming or outgoing calls by clicking on the Recent Calls button and choosing the number.

CHANGING CONVERSATION PLACE DEFAULTS

You will need to set some options for Conversation Place to properly dial. Figure 16.3 shows the Location Information dialog box where you set the area code and necessary numbers for outside line access (an example: dialing 9 for an outside line). If you travel with a laptop and plan to use Conversation Place on it, you should set up several locations, one for each city you plan to travel to. To access the Location Information dialog box, follow these steps:

1. Choose Edit Menu and Locations. Create at least one location by filling in a name, area code, and special access numbers if they exist.

2. Once you have completed the location setup, click OK.

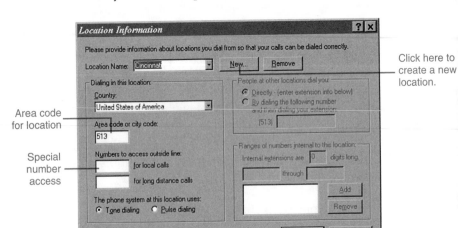

Click here to create a new location.

Area code for location

Special number access

FIGURE 16.3 The Conversation Place Location Information dialog box.

SETTING MORE OPTIONS

Conversation Place also has an Options command that allows you to:

- Set up a default voice-mail number.

- Choose the name you want Conversation Place to display in the main window.

- Choose the sound that Conversation Place plays when alerting you of incoming calls.

Follow these steps to set Conversation Place options.

1. In the Conversation Place application window (see Figure 16.1) choose the Tools menu and the Options command. The Options dialog box appears (see Figure 16.4).

2. Set the Name, Voice-mail, and Sound on Incoming calls options and click OK. You may have to browse for the sound file by choosing the **Browse** button. If so, you will be taken to the Select Sound File dialog box to search for a sound file.

 Sound Files?   They're not included with GroupWise 5 or Conversation Place. You can use any sound file (such as a WAV or MIDI sound) that already exists on your hard drive, but you will need to know what directories they are stored in so you can browse and find them.

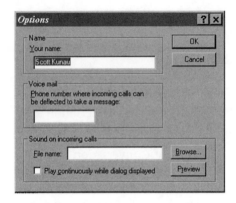

FIGURE 16.4   The Options dialog box.

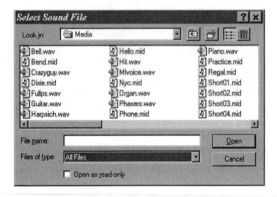

FIGURE 16.5   The Select Sound File dialog box.

SETTING UP CONFERENCE CALLS

You can use Conversation Place to start conference calls, bring two or more outside calls together into a conference, transfer a call, disconnect calls, or put a caller on hold. You can also use a combination of these features. For example, if you are talking to one caller while you have another caller on hold and you realize all three of you need to be in the same conversation, instead of hanging up on one caller and calling back to conference, you can simply merge the calls. If you have more than two active conversations, Conversation Place lets you choose the conversations you want to merge. Follow these steps to place or set up a conference call:

1. With at least one caller on the line, either in an active conversation or on hold, click Conference.

2. Type the name of the person in the Enter Name box until the correct name appears. Or browse through the address book to find the correct user.

3. When the user's name (the person who will join the conference) appears in the name and phone number fields, click Dial.

In this lesson you learned about the Conversation Place application that accompanies GroupWise 5. You also learned how to set options and locations and place calls using your personal address book and Conversation Place. In the next lesson you will learn how to use the remote features of GroupWise 5.

USING GROUPWISE 5 REMOTELY

In this lesson you'll learn how to work with GroupWise 5 remotely from your laptop while you're out of the office.

SETTING UP TO ACCESS GROUPWISE 5 REMOTE

Out on the road, using a laptop, you are obviously not going to be connected to your company's GroupWise 5 system. When you send messages, they will be stored on the laptop hard drive until you can reconnect your laptop to the GroupWise 5 system. Your system administrator will likely have configured a modem for use with your laptop so you can dial into the company network and access GroupWise 5. If the system administrator has not enabled your laptop for dial-in access, and you plan to be on the road for a few days, you may want to get a modem and have the administrator configure your laptop to use it for dial-in access to pick up your GroupWise 5 messages on a daily basis.

Creating and sending messages with GroupWise 5 Remote is identical to sending messages with the network version of GroupWise 5 software. GroupWise 5 will automatically try to connect to the GroupWise 5 system and if it cannot, you will be prompted with the GroupWise 5 startup dialog box (see Figure 17.1).

If GroupWise 5 cannot connect to the company network and the GroupWise 5 system, the remote portion of GroupWise 5 will automatically start. You will be shown your user name, you will likely be prompted for your mailbox password, and you may be required to search for the remote database location on your laptop hard drive. The location of the remote database directory should already appear because your system administrator will have configured your laptop prior to giving it to you.

If your remote mailbox has a password on it, enter that password. The path to your remote database should appear in the Path to remote database field. If no path appears, you will have to use the Browse button and search through the directory structure on your laptop for it (see Figure 17.1). Click OK to continue accessing GroupWise 5 Remote.

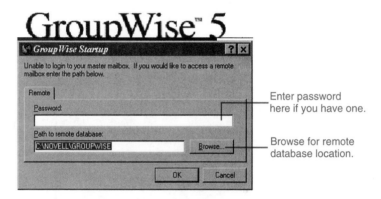

Enter password here if you have one.

Browse for remote database location.

FIGURE 17.1   The GroupWise 5 Remote Startup dialog box.

USING YOUR REMOTE MAILBOX

Your remote mailbox looks almost identical to your master mailbox in the system. There is one additional menu command for you to choose: The Remote menu. Before you leave the office with your laptop, you need to synchronize or replicate the master mailbox (which resides on the network) with your remote mailbox located on your laptop's hard drive. Synchronizing the two mailboxes enables you to copy the following to your remote database: the system address book, all of your folders, rules, and of course, all of the messages stored in your master mailbox. In order to update or synchronize your remote mailbox with your master mailbox, follow these steps:

1. While you are connected and logged into the company network, start GroupWise 5 from your laptop. You will know you are connected and using the network version of GroupWise 5 because of the absence of a Remote menu command. Choose the Tools menu and the Hit the Road command. You will be prompted to enter a password for your mailbox, if one exists.

2. If a password exists, enter your master mailbox password in the password dialog box and click OK. The Retrieve Options dialog box appears for you to choose what items to update as shown in Figure 17.2.

3. Choose the items you want to update to your remote mailbox by clicking the boxes next to each. Click the Finish button to start the update process.

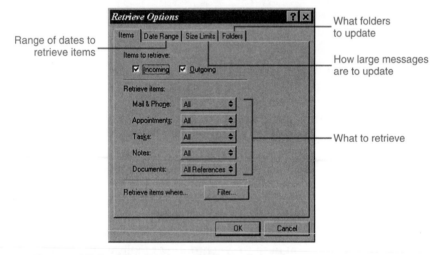

FIGURE 17.2 The Retrieve Options dialog box.

4. Choose any of the following options for retrieving messages from your master mailbox:

   • **Items** Choose the types of messages you want to retrieve. Typically, you should leave this screen at default and update all types of messages.

- **Date Range** Choose a range of dates to limit which messages are retrieved. By default you will go back 5 days and you will go forward by 365 days.

- **Size Limits** Choose how large messages are that you want to retrieve. Larger messages take a lot of time when downloading them over a modem (thus the reason for connecting to your network prior to leaving the office to update). You can specify to get the subject line only of your messages; get the messages regardless of their size; or get the messages based on a size criteria. If you choose to get the subject line only, you will then have to select the actual messages to retrieve and go through the Hit the Road steps an additional time.

- **Folders** Choose which folders to retrieve. If you choose the retrieve folders, and the folders do not already exist in your remote mailbox, the folders and all of their contents will be synchronized to your remote mailbox.

5. Click OK when you are done making choices from the Retrieve Options dialog box.

6. You will see GroupWise 5 make a Hit the Road connection to update your remote mailbox. Wait for the connection to finish. You will be returned to your GroupWise 5 mailbox automatically, where you can exit the program and shut down your Windows 95 laptop, in preparation to leave the office.

Hit the Road Update It is much faster to connect your laptop to the network and use the Hit the Road command than it is to try and synchronize your master mailbox and remote mailbox via a dial-up connection.

SEND MESSAGES FROM GROUPWISE 5 REMOTE

In GroupWise 5 Remote, you create and send messages, create rules and folders, and use the address book in the same manner as if you are connected to the network.

Whenever you make a remote connection to the GroupWise 5 system, all messages you have created while in remote mode are automatically sent and stored in your remote mailbox on your laptop. You can't choose to send some messages and not others; you can only specify what to retrieve.

The only real difference is that you won't be able to receive messages as they are sent; you will need to reconnect to the GroupWise 5 system to receive new messages (see the task earlier in this lesson).

1. Create and send a new message (see Lesson 4). When you are ready to connect to the GroupWise 5 system, choose the Remote menu and the Send/Retrieve command. You will see the dialog box shown in Figure 17.3. However, as shown in Figure 17.3, you will see there is one message waiting to be sent. You cannot choose what messages to send from your remote mailbox to your master mailbox, but you can choose what items to retrieve. Both the send and the retrieve operations are completed each time you connect to your GroupWise 5 system.

2. To specify different items to retrieve, click the Advanced button. You will see the Retrieve Options dialog box (see Figure 17.2).

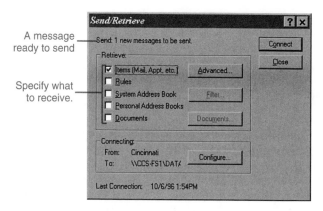

A message ready to send

Specify what to receive.

FIGURE 17.3   The Send/Retrieve dialog box.

A REMINDER TO UPDATE THE MASTER MAILBOX

Another powerful GroupWise 5 feature is its capability to detect when you have been working in remote mode. If you have been away from the office and using GroupWise 5 remotely, you will be prompted to update your master mailbox when you reconnect the remote computer to the network and access GroupWise 5 (see Figure 17.4). If you completed a dial-in connection and updated your master mailbox prior to connecting your laptop back into the company network in your office, you will not see this message.

TIP

Automatic Remote Processing   You have the option to have GroupWise 5 process the requests you completed while in remote mode without prompting you. To make your requests automatic, click the Don't display this prompt again box and then click Yes.

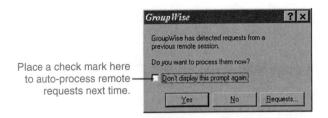

Place a check mark here to auto-process remote requests next time.

FIGURE 17.4   A dialog box reminding you of a remote session.

As soon as you click Yes to process the remote messages and other events you completed while in remote mode, GroupWise 5 will make a "Smart Docking" Network Connection (see Figure 17.5). In other words, you don't have to worry how to get GroupWise 5 remote connected in order to process your work. The Smart Docking Network Connection will be made if you run GroupWise 5 (in normal mode) on the same computer you used to remotely access GroupWise 5. Your requests will be uploaded and handled by the GroupWise 5 system. Once the update process is done, you will be ready to work in GroupWise 5 network mode.

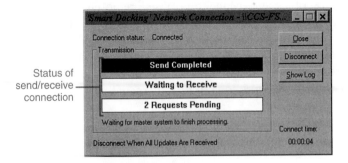

Status of send/receive connection

FIGURE 17.5   The Smart Docking Network Connection dialog box.

When you are out in the field and working in remote mode, you will follow the same procedures and see the same dialog boxes as those pictured in this lesson. The only difference is that when you are out in the field, you will first have to dial into your company's

GroupWise 5 system with a telephone and computer modem. Your GroupWise 5 system administrator will have to set up this hardware prior to you working in the field with GroupWise 5 Remote.

In this lesson you learned how to work with GroupWise 5 Remote, how to Hit the Road and update your remote mailbox and finally how to send and receive remote messages. In the next lesson, you will learn how to create and send Internet references.

18

CREATING AND SENDING INTERNET REFERENCES

In this lesson you'll learn how to create and send Internet References with GroupWise 5. You will also learn how to store an Internet reference message in your mailbox for future reference.

WHAT ARE INTERNET REFERENCES?

So, you want to hit a cool Internet Web site, but you don't know the Universal Resource Locator (URL)? GroupWise 5 offers you the ability to create, store, and send references to Internet locations (World Wide Web pages and FTP sites). The addresses or references used are often referred to as URLs.

In order to access the Internet from your PC, you will need a modem to connect to an Internet service provider (ISP) or other method to actually make an Internet connection, such as a direct network connection within your company. You will also need Internet browser software like the Netscape Navigator or Microsoft's Internet Explorer.

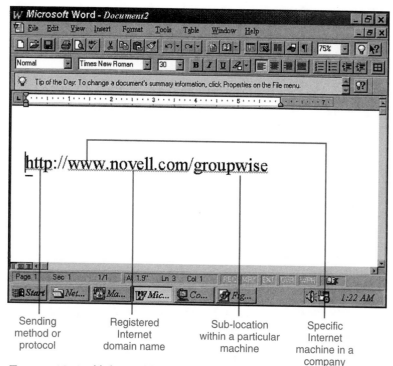

Sending   Registered   Sub-location   Specific
method or   Internet   within a particular   Internet
protocol   domain name   machine   machine in a
                                                      company

FIGURE 18.1   Universal Resource Locator.

CREATING AND STORING INTERNET REFERENCES

There are millions of files in thousands of locations on the Internet. If you have several locations, or Web pages as they are sometimes called, that you regularly access, or you want to share these locations (URLs) with other GroupWise 5 users, you should create and store these locations in your own mailbox and consider sending them to other users. By storing or sending the Internet references, you simplify access to specific locations on the Internet. Follow these steps to create an Internet Reference and store it in your mailbox:

1. Click the Cabinet Folder or one of the other folders of your mailbox, other than the mailbox folder itself.

Internet Reference and the Mailbox   You cannot create an Internet Reference in your mailbox. You can receive and store one in it, however.

2. Choose the Tools menu. Click the Internet command, then click Create Internet Location. This brings up the Create Internet Reference dialog box (see Figure 18.2).

3. Type the Internet address location into the Internet Location box. Press Tab and type a subject that describes the location and click OK.

Type the Internet location here.   Paste Location button

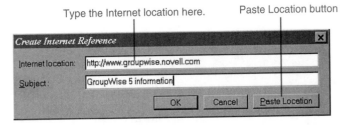

FIGURE **18.2**   The Create Internet Reference dialog box.

Pasting Internet Location   You can use the Paste Location button to paste an Internet location into the Internet References dialog box provided you have the address already available in another application. Copy the address from the other application, position your cursor in the Internet location field and then choose the Paste Location button.

4. Click OK to save the Internet reference into the folder you selected prior to creating it. The Internet reference will be stored, like a message, in one of your folders.

SENDING AN INTERNET REFERENCE

Suppose you find a particularly valuable Internet location and you want to share it with other GroupWise 5 users. This Internet location may already exist in your own mailbox or it may be a new one you just learned about. Follow these steps to send an Internet reference to another user:

 1. Choose the Tools menu. Click the Internet command, then click Send Internet Location. This brings up the Send Internet Location dialog box (see Figure 18.3). You can also click the Send Internet Reference button on the Toolbar.

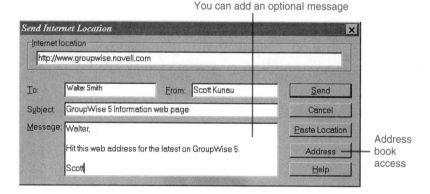

FIGURE 18.3   The Send Internet Location dialog box.

2. Type the Internet location into the Internet location box.

3. Type the recipients' addresses into the TO: box or click the Address button to open the Address Book where you choose users.

4. Type a subject and an optional message and click Send.

RECEIVING AND USING AN INTERNET LOCATION

After you receive a message with an Internet location message it, or you have created an Internet location in your own mailbox, you need to open it in order to access the Internet location. Follow these steps to use an Internet location.

1. Open your mailbox to display the Internet location message (see Figure 18.4). Double-click on the Internet location message in your mailbox to open the message containing the Internet location (see Figure 18.5).

Target folder for
Internet references   Internet references

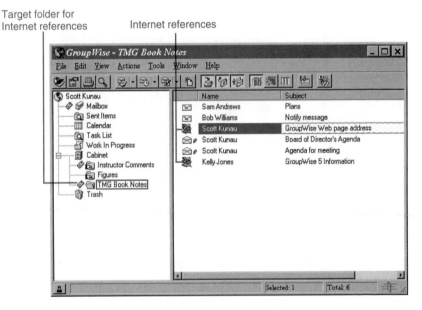

FIGURE 18.4 The Mailbox shows Internet location messages.

Go to Internet location

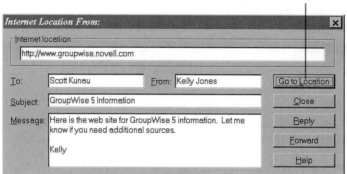

FIGURE 18.5   Incoming Internet Reference message.

2. If this is an Internet address you want to access, click Go to Location. GroupWise 5 will cause your browser to run so you can access the Internet and the URL stored in the Internet location message (see Figure 18.6).

3. If you'd rather not open the Web page to which the Internet location refers, you can close, reply, or forward it to another user.

Internet location

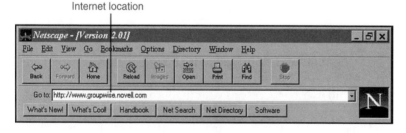

FIGURE 18.6   Internet access software.

In this lesson you learned how to create, store, send, and use Internet references to access the Internet. In the next lesson you will learn how to access another user's mailbox.

LESSON 19

ACCESSING ANOTHER'S MAILBOX

In this chapter you'll learn how to access another user's mailbox with the Proxy feature. You will also learn how to grant access to another user so that user can access your mailbox.

USING THE PROXY FEATURE

Proxy Your ability to read and possibly manage another user's mailbox and calendar from your own GroupWise 5 mailbox. The other user must personally grant you access to his mailbox. He can give you read or write access to his mail and phone, tasks, notes, and appointment messages. Once you are granted this ability, you can read and possibly reply, forward, delegate, and delete their messages.

Accessing another GroupWise 5 user's mailbox is made easy with the Proxy feature, as long as the user has granted you access. By default, no user has access to your mailbox; you have to give permission to enable others to view and/or manage your mailbox and calendar. You will first learn about the types of access rights and how to grant them, and then you will learn how to gain access to another user's GroupWise 5 mailbox using the Proxy feature.

GRANTING ACCESS TO ANOTHER USER

Minimum User Access The Proxy feature of GroupWise includes the Minimum User Access you can use to grant access to read and/or write items on your calendar and in your mailbox. Granting access rights to Minimum User Access provides those rights to *every* GroupWise user in your system.

In order for another user to read items in your mailbox or on your calendar, you must first grant them the ability to do so through Proxy access rights. You can grant different types of rights to different users or grant minimum access to all of the GroupWise 5 users in your system.

1. Within your GroupWise 5 mailbox, choose the Tools menu and the Options command. This will take you into the GroupWise 5 Options dialog box (see Figure 19.1).

Security icon; start proxy access here.

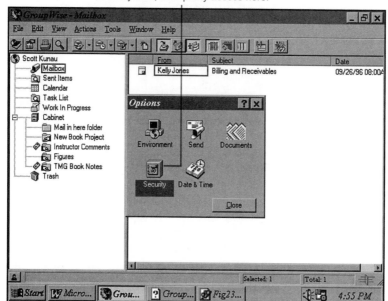

FIGURE 19.1   The GroupWise 5 Options dialog box.

2. Double-click the Security icon. This will take you to the
   Security Options dialog box (see Figure 19.2). (You will
   learn about the other options in Lesson 21.)

3. Click on the Proxy Access tab. The first time you choose
   this tab, only Minimum User Access will appear in the
   Access list. After you add users to the list, they will appear
   in the Access list.

 Regranting Access If you grant proxy access to a user
and that user's GroupWise 5 user ID changes (by being
moved or renamed), you will have to grant access to the
user again or they will not be able to proxy your mailbox.

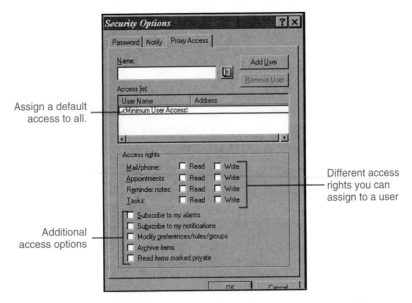

Assign a default
access to all.

Additional
access options

Different access
rights you can
assign to a user

Figure 19.2 The Security Options dialog where you grant Proxy
Access.

4. To add users to the Access list, click the address book
   icon, then double-click each user you want to grant access
   to. Repeat this step for each user you want to add to the
   Access list.

> **Type the Username** If you know the user ID of the person you want to grant proxy access to, type their user ID into the Name box and click on the Add User button. They will be added to the Access List.

Types of proxy access and the items you can grant access to:

- **Read** Allows a user to read selected items in your mailbox. Items include mail and phone, tasks, notes, and appointment messages.

- **Write** Allows a user to take action on a selected item in your mailbox. Actions include reply, delete, delegate, reply, accept, or decline.

- **Subscribe to my alarms** Allows another user to receive the same alarms you receive.

- **Subscribe to my notifications** Allows another user to receive notification that you have received new messages.

- **Modify preferences/rules/groups** Allows the user to modify all of your GroupWise 5 settings and options; grant or modify proxy access to your mailbox; create and modify the rules you have created.

- **Archive items** Allows another user to archive your messages into his archive folder, making them inaccessible to you.

- **Read items marked private** Allows another user to read messages sent to you that the sender marked as private. A privately marked message will not appear in your mailbox when a proxy user is reading messages, unless that user has been granted the ability to read items marked private.

5. To grant access rights, select a user in the Access List then click the check boxes next to each access right you want him to have. These will include: **Read** or **Write** to **Mail/phone**, **Appointments**, **Reminder notes**, and **Tasks**.

You can also allow a user to subscribe to your alarms and notifications, modify your GroupWise 5 preferences, archive items for you and read private items (see the list above for a complete description of each).

 Don't Grant These Think carefully before granting a proxy user access to archive items and to read items marked as private access. Doing so might make your messages inaccessible to you if the proxy user archives the messages. Also, if a proxy user is granted access to read items marked private, you eliminate any confidentiality the sender may have intended, as the proxy user will see your private messages.

6. When you are done granting access to users, click OK to return to the Options dialog box. Click Close in the Options dialog box to return to your mailbox.

7. **(Optional)** If you need to remove a user from the Access rights list, choose the Tools menu, Security icon, select the Proxy Access tab, choose the user and click on the Remove User button. Click OK to exit the Security Options dialog box and then Close to return to your mailbox.

USING PROXY

Once you have been granted proxy access to other users' GroupWise 5 mailboxes, you can use the Proxy feature to access their mailboxes to read and possibly to take action on their messages. Follow these steps to use the Proxy feature.

1. Choose the File menu and the Proxy command. This will bring the Proxy dialog box up on your screen (see Figure 19.3).

2. Click on the address book icon near the OK button to access the main GroupWise 5 address book.

3. Choose the user who has given you access to serve as a proxy for their mailbox and click OK.

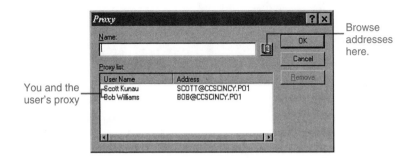

Browse addresses here.

You and the user's proxy

FIGURE 19.3 The Proxy dialog box with one additional user proxied.

 Access Denied? If you receive an error message when you click OK to leave the Proxy dialog box, you will know you have not been granted access to proxy the user you chose from the address book.

4. Click the user from the Proxy list and click OK. Your mailbox will soon become their mailbox, where you will be able to see and read their messages.

5. To return to your own mailbox, choose the File menu and the Proxy command, choose yourself from the Proxy list and click OK.

 Button to Proxy Access Once you have added a user to your proxy list, via the File menu and the Proxy command, you can quickly proxy that user's mailbox by clicking on the Proxy pop-up list icon located in the lower-left corner of most GroupWise 5 views.

In this lesson you learned how to set up access to your mailbox for other users to serve as proxy for you. You also learned how to use the proxy feature of GroupWise 5. In the next lesson you will learn about setting up rules for your mailbox.

LESSON 20

CREATING AND USING RULES

In this chapter you'll learn how to create a rule to help you automate message organization.

WHAT ARE RULES?

Rules Groupwise 5 rules are used to define a set of conditions and actions to be performed when an item or action meets those conditions. You can specify actions such as moving items to folders, forwarding and replying to items, and more. Rules can help you organize your Mailbox, automate your Mailbox when you are away, or delete unwanted items.

You have learned to create folders to help you organize your GroupWise 5 mailbox. In this chapter you will learn why rules should be used and how to create rules to help you manage your mailbox with those folders.

Rules are an effective way to automate messages that you receive, send, partially complete, accept, or simply want to file away prior to archiving (see Lesson 6 for more about archiving messages). For example, you can create rules to automate the sending of a new mail message, to store certain types of messages you receive in a specific folder, to delegate a task to another user, or even to forward certain messages to another user.

You can also create a rule to handle personal messages such as personal tasks, personal appointments, or personal notes, as well as draft items that you are working on but are not ready to send.

CREATING A RULE TO FILE MESSAGES INTO FOLDERS

As you use the GroupWise 5 mailbox more and more, you'll find yourself doing some tasks repeatedly. For example, when you open the mailbox you'll probably see certain messages (messages with a particular subject or from a particular person) that you want to keep in a specific folder. In this situation you can create a simple rule that will save you time.

1. From your GroupWise 5 mailbox, choose the Tools menu and the Rules command to open the Rules dialog box as shown in Figure 20.1.

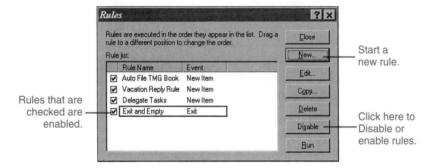

FIGURE 20.1   The Rules dialog box showing several rules.

2. Choose New to create a new rule and open the New Rule dialog box (see Figure 20.2).

3. Name the Rule.

 TIP   **Naming Rules**   Give the rule a short, descriptive name that explains what it does. Later when you learn how to disable the rule, it will be easy to pick which one(s) to disable by looking at the Rule Name in the Rules dialog box. You learn to disable a rule later in this lesson.

Name the rule

Choose the items to which the rule applies

What message types will be affected by the rule

Actions to take

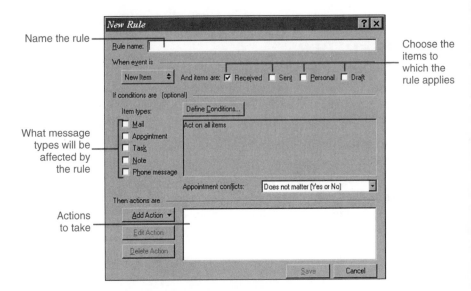

Figure 20.2 The New Rule dialog box.

4. Decide what message items will be affected: **Received**, **Sent**, **Personal**, and/or **Draft** items and click to add a check mark to those you want to affect.

 Personal and Draft Items Messages that are personal to you (i.e. personal tasks, notes, and appointments) or messages you are currently working on but are not ready to send.

5. If you want a particular type of message to be affected by the rule, check the appropriate Item types.

 TIP **A Rule for All Messages** If you want all messages to be handled by the rule, leave all of the boxes unchecked in the New Rule dialog box.

6. Click the Add Action button under Then actions are area of the New Rule dialog box. You can choose to:

- **Move a message to a folder**   Moves messages to folders you have created first and then selected for this action.

- **Reply to sender**   Automatically sends a reply, composed during the creation of the rule, to the sender of the message.

- **Delegate a message**   Sends a task, note, or appointment on to a pre-selected user. For example, while you are on vacation, you can delegate a person to be backup and set up a rule to delegate all incoming tasks, notes, and appointments to them.

- **Delete or decline a message received**   When rule conditions are met, the incoming item will be deleted or declined. You might use a rule to decline appointments on certain days when you are always in meetings.

- **Archive a message**   Starts the archive process on the message when rule conditions are met.

- **Empty item**   Automatically empties the item from your Trash folder when the rule conditions are met.

- **Send mail**   Sends a message you compose during the creation of the rule. This message goes to anyone you address it to when the rule executes.

- **Forward a message**   Forwards the incoming message, when the rule conditions are met, to one or more recipients.

- **Accept the message**   Automatically accepts the task, note, or appointment.

- **Mark the message as private**   A private message cannot be read by a user who can proxy your mailbox. (See Lesson 19 on Proxy.)

- **Mark the message as read or unread** Marks a message read (or unread) even though you may not have done so. This is handy for discussion threads you may not want to follow. The automatic feature will tag the discussion messages as read so they won't sort at the top of an item list.

- **Stop rule processing** If rule conditions are met, this action will halt further actions that might be applied on a message.

7. Choose the Move To Folder command. The Move Item to Folder Action dialog box appears (see Figure 20.3) displaying the various folders you can choose to move the message into. Choose a folder by clicking in the box to the left of the folder name and then click Move.

8. To finish the rule, click the Save button in the New Rule dialog box. Click Close from the Rules dialog box to return to your mailbox.

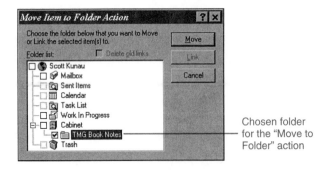

Chosen folder for the "Move to Folder" action

Figure 20.3 The Move Item to Folder Action dialog box showing folders to move the message into.

CREATING AN AUTOMATIC REPLY RULE

In the last task, we created a rule that automatically files certain incoming messages into one of your folders. Let's say that you have decided to add another action to this rule which will cause an automatic reply to occur. Follow these steps to edit an existing rule.

1. From your GroupWise 5 mailbox, choose the Tools menu and the Rules command to open the Rules dialog box (see Figure 20.1). Select the rule you want to add an action to and click the Edit button.

2. Click the Add Action button and choose Reply. The Reply dialog box appears. Check the Reply to Sender radio button and **(optionally)** Check **Message Received From Sender** to remind the sender what you are replying to and click OK. (See Lesson 6 for a review on replying to a sender.)

Can't Change To: You cannot change the user ID in the To: text box because you are replying to the sender's original message, not creating a new message to the original sender.

3. Type in a short reply and click OK. Save the rule by clicking the Save button in the Edit Rule dialog box. You will be returned to the Rules dialog box. Click the Close button to return to your mailbox.

Which Recipients?   You should typically auto-reply, in your rule, only to the sender of an incoming message to avoid sending unnecessary messages through the system. It is unlikely that multiple recipients of the original message will need to see your auto-reply message generated by the rule. Therefore you should select **Reply to All** only if you feel all recipients need to see your reply.

> **No Auto-reply**   You likely will not want your rule to auto-reply to incoming Internet messages. Placing a **!** prior to the **@** symbol will prevent automatic replies to Internet messages and will help your GroupWise 5 system function better by not overloading it with automatic replies. This is especially important if you receive a lot of Internet mail.

Disabling an Active Rule

Your rule has been active and has done its job effectively. Now you want to disable the rule, but not delete it.

1. From your mailbox, choose the Tools menu and the Rules command. This will open the Rules dialog box (see Figure 20.1).

2. To deactivate or disable a rule, simply click on the check box to remove the check mark. (See Figure 20.4.) You can also select a rule in the Rule list and choose the Disable button (see Figure 20.1).

3. Click the Close button to return to your mailbox.

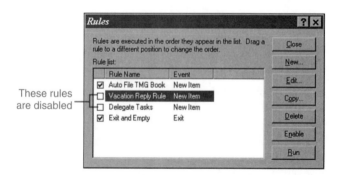

These rules are disabled

Figure 20.4   The Rules dialog box showing disabled rules.

In this lesson you learned how to create a rule to automatically move messages to a folder, how to use a rule to reply to a sender, and how to disable a rule. In the next lesson you will learn how to customize GroupWise 5.

LESSON 21

CUSTOMIZING GROUPWISE 5

In this lesson you'll learn to customize the GroupWise 5 environment, to change send options for all messages, to sort messages, change mailbox properties, and to set a password on your GroupWise 5 mailbox.

Your default setup for GroupWise 5 specifies views for each message type, basic cleanup options, no password on your mailbox, and no proxy access for other users.

CHANGING THE GROUPWISE 5 DEFAULT SETTINGS

When you first open GroupWise 5, you will more than likely have a default configuration. The GroupWise 5 default configuration means that the way in which information is displayed in your mailbox, the directories in which information is saved and archived, and the way messages are sent and received are preset to the options that most users find convenient. After you've worked with GroupWise 5 a while, you may decide that these default settings really don't suit your methods.

You change the GroupWise 5 environment from the Environment dialog box. Here is a summary of the options available to you:

- **General tab**   Controls default actions on messages, attachments and view options. A handy setting here is read next after delete, accept or decline a message.

- **Views tab**   Controls the default view that appears when you send a new message.

- **File Location tab**   Controls where the archive directory, the save directory, the check-out directory, and the custom views directory are located on either your hard drive or on the network.

- **Cleanup tab**   Controls the message archive and deletion of messages in your mailbox and Trash can.

- **Signature tab**   Controls what signature and closing you want added to each message you send. The default is Off.

To change your GroupWise 5 environment, follow these steps:

1. Choose the Tools menu and the Options command. This will bring up the Options dialog box (see Figure 21.1).

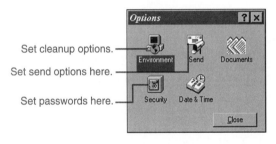

FIGURE 21.1   The Options dialog box.

2. Double-click the Environment icon and open the Environment dialog box. The General tab is in front by default. Here you can change the language, view options, default actions, and the handling of attachments.

3. Click the Views tab to display it (see Figure 21.2). To change the default view that is displayed each time you open GroupWise 5, click one of the options under the Item type. Once you have selected the new default view, click on the Set Default View button.

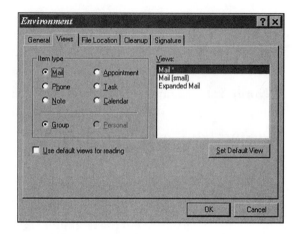

FIGURE 21.2   The Environment dialog box showing the Views tab.

4. Click the File Location tab (see Figure 21.3) to set or change default directories for your Archive directory (see Lesson 6), your Save, check-out directory, and your Custom views directory.

Archive Directory   Holds the archive databases for your mailbox.

Custom Views Directory   Holds all of the custom views you create with the GroupWise 5 view designer.

Save, check-out Directory   Holds any messages or documents you want to save to files outside of the GroupWise 5 system.

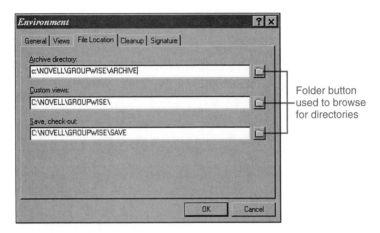

Folder button
used to browse
for directories

FIGURE 21.3   The File Location tab showing the directories for storing files.

5. Click once on the Cleanup tab to show all of the cleanup options you or the system administrator can apply to your mailbox.

You Must Clean House   Proper "care" of your GroupWise 5 mailbox is essential in order to avoid message problems. By archiving or deleting your messages and regularly emptying your trash, you can help the administrator solve GroupWise 5 problems before they start.

6. Choose how often you want your mail and phone messages either automatically archived or deleted from your mailbox. Also, choose how often your tasks, notes, and appointments should be archived or deleted and how often your trash can should be purged automatically (see Lesson 7 on working with the trash). When you are done, click OK.

To Close Together   Don't set the delete message options too close to the empty trash options otherwise messages may be deleted and purged before you can read them.

Options Are Gray?   If the cleanup options (or any other options in the Environment or other dialog boxes are gray, it is because your system administrator has set the options and locked them to prevent users from changing the settings.

Mail, phone, appointments, tasks, and note options are set to manual delete by default.

Messages are purged after 7 days by default.

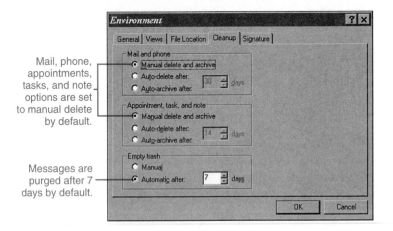

FIGURE 21.4   The Cleanup options tab showing default settings.

7. When you have completed setting Environment options, click OK and then click Close (X).

CHANGING SEND OPTIONS

We learned in Lesson 4 how to set the send options for the current message. In this lesson we learn how to set the options for every message you send.

To change send options for all the message types you send, choose Tools, Options from the menu, then double-click the Send icon. The Send Options dialog box appears (see Figure 21.5).

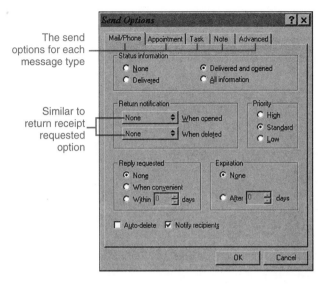

The send
options for each
message type

Similar to
return receipt
requested
option

FIGURE 21.5   The Send Options dialog box showing the default
send options.

You will see a tab for each message type (Mail/Phone, Appointment, and so on). Simply click the tab of the message type whose
send options you want to change and then click the appropriate
options to activate or deactivate them. Here is a summary of what
you can change for each message type:

Status information   Allows you to track delivery results
of sent messages (see Lesson 8).

Return notification   Is similar to sending a letter with
"return receipt requested."

Priority   Lets you change how a message will look in the
recipient's mailbox. Using high priority may move the message through the GroupWise 5 system slightly faster, depending upon how your system administrator has the
system configured.

Reply requested   Places a reminder at the top of the message box asking the recipient to reply.

Expiration   Will remove an unopened message from a
recipient's mailbox upon expiration.

Auto-delete   Will delete your messages from the Sent Items folder when all recipients have deleted the message.

Notify recipients   Will trigger Notify to alert a recipient a message has arrived (see Lesson 22).

Changing Your Password

Company policy may require that you have a password on your mailbox. Or, you may need to put a password on your mailbox so you can use the Hit the Road remote feature (see Lesson 17). Your GroupWise 5 password will be different from your network password and once you set your GroupWise 5 password, it will be required each time you start GroupWise 5.

When you create a password for yourself, you should keep the following in mind:

- Don't use names of family members or commonly known dates. Anyone who knows you and wants to access your mailbox could probably figure out your password without much trouble.

- Make your password a combination of at least five letters and numbers. The longer the password is, the harder it will be to figure out.

- If you forget your password, your system administrator will have to remove it so you can set a new one.

- Don't leave your password on a post-it note stuck to your monitor. You should always memorize your password, but if you can't, write it down and store it in a safe place.

- All GroupWise 5 passwords are case-sensitive. When creating a password, using a combination of upper- and lowercase letters as well as symbols will make the password difficult to guess.

To create your password:

1. Choose the Tools menu and the Options command. Then double-click the Security icon to open the Security Options dialog box (see Figure 21.6).

2. Type your password in the New password: box and press Tab to move to the Confirm new password: box. Retype the password in this box.

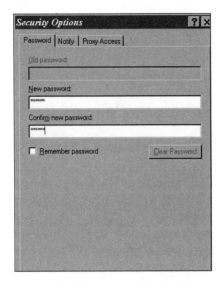

FIGURE 21.6   The Security Options dialog box showing a new password being set.

SORTING YOUR MAILBOX

Instead of having a myriad of items mixed up in your mailbox, you can sort your mailbox and make items appear in a more organized fashion. Follow these steps to change the order of how your messages are displayed:

1. Choose the View menu and the Sort command. This opens the Sort dialog box as seen in Figure 21.7.

2. In the Sort by: list, select the criteria by which you want your messages sorted. In the Order area, click either Ascending or Descending depending upon how you want to sort items.

3. Click OK and notice how your mailbox appears in a different order.

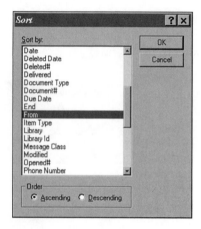

FIGURE 21.7   The Sort dialog box.

CHANGING MAILBOX PROPERTIES AND CREATING CUSTOM VIEWS

You may want to change the default properties for viewing and sorting your mailbox. You have the option to change which folder is opened when GroupWise 5 starts. You can control which columns of information appear, the order in which they appear, and the amount of space they take up on your display.

If you decide you like the changes you've made to the display of your mailbox, you can save these changes as a *custom display*.

Follow these steps to change the properties of your mailbox and create a custom display.

1. Click the top level of your GroupWise 5 mailbox. This is called the user folder and it is where your name appears at the top of the folder structure.

2. Choose the File menu and the Properties command. The Properties dialog box will appear. Click the Display tab (see Figure 21.8). You can also right-click on the user folder and click on Properties.

3. Select the Setting name that you want to affect, then select how to view and sort that particular folder. You can
also indicate which items will appear in a particular
folder.

4. **(Optional)** If you want to save these settings as a custom
display, choose the Save As... command, provide a new
settings name in the Display settings Save As dialog box
and click OK.

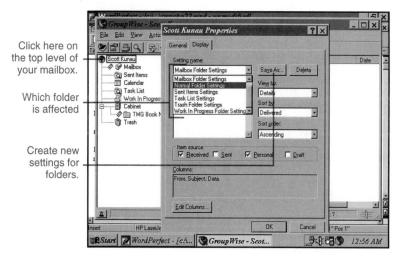

Click here on
the top level of
your mailbox.

Which folder
is affected

Create new
settings for
folders.

FIGURE 21.8   The Properties dialog box with the Display tab
showing.

5. To apply the new settings without saving them, click OK.

In this lesson you learned how to set a variety of environment
options on your GroupWise 5 mailbox: how to set send options
to affect every message you send, how to set a password on your
GroupWise 5 mailbox, how to sort your mailbox, and how to
change mailbox properties. In the next lesson, you will learn how
to use the Notify feature.

USING NOTIFY

In this lesson you'll learn how to start and use the GroupWise 5 Notify program, how to change the options for the program and how to read a GroupWise 5 message that you have been notified about.

GroupWise 5 Notify is an extra utility you can run to alert you to the fact that new messages have arrived in your mailbox. You can start the program running automatically each time you start Windows, or you can manually run the program after Windows is running. You will notice that Notify runs minimized as a Windows 95 task bar icon. Only when you have new mail in your mailbox does Notify "come alive" and alert you about the new message.

No Auto-Notify? Access to Notify is installed on your computer but must be set up by your system administrator in order to run automatically each time you start Windows.

STARTING AND USING NOTIFY

To start the Notify program manually, follow these steps.

1. Open the Novell GroupWise 5 folder from the Start menu. The Novell GroupWise 5 folder appears (see Figure 22.1).

2. Double-click the Notify icon. You will see the initial startup screen for Notify and then you will notice the program icon appear in the lower-right corner of your Windows 95 taskbar.

FIGURE 22.1   The Novell GroupWise 5 folder.

The Notify Program Icon

FIGURE 22.2   When Notify is running, look for the icon on the taskbar.

You will learn how to respond to a Notify alert later in this lesson.

CHANGING THE NOTIFY OPTIONS

Notify is a taskbar icon and therefore, you must click on the icon located on the taskbar in order to change the options for the program. When you open the Notify Options dialog box, you will see several tabs that identify the options you can change:

- **General tab**   Controls which folders Notify monitors for new messages and how often it looks for those messages. You can also control how long the Notify dialog box appears on the screen alerting you of new messages.

- **Notify tab**   Controls music that Notify plays, controls whether the Notify dialog box appears and allows you to set up a program that will launch when a messages arrive based upon a specified priority and message type.

- **Alarms tab**   Controls the music Notify plays, whether the Notify dialog box opens and which program launches when an appointment alarm sounds.

- **Return Status tab**   Controls how you are notified of various status changes in messages you send.

Follow these steps to change your Notify options.

1. Right-click the Notify icon on the taskbar.

2. Choose Options from the quick menu. This will open your Notify Options dialog box (see Figure 22.3). Here you will see four tabs: General, Notify, Alarm, and Return Status.

3. In the General tab, choose which of your GroupWise 5 folders you want Notify to monitor. If you want Notify to monitor several folders, select the first folder then press the Ctrl key and click on each folder to select it. In the settings area, choose how often you want Notify to scan your mailbox and how long you want the notification dialog to remain on your computer screen.

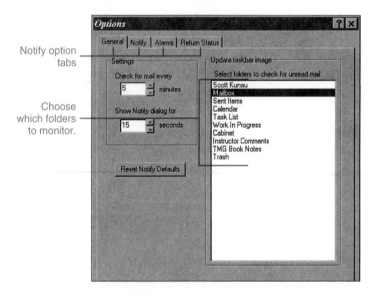

FIGURE 22.3 The Notify Options dialog box.

4. Click the Notify tab (see Figure 22.4). Check the options you want to have Notify alert you with in the event of a new message arrival. You can specify different types of notification for the different messages (mail, phone, task, and so on) sent through GroupWise 5.

To have Notify alert you with a sound, position your cursor in the Play Sound box on each of the message priority boxes and then click on the Browse directory button to search for a sound file. Be sure to deselect the Use same settings for all types check box or you won't be able to select different alerts for different messages.

5. Click on the Alarms tab. Set the type of alarm, whether the Notify dialog box will appear and which application (if any) will launch when an appointment alarm sounds.

6. Click the Return Status tab. Set Notify alerts here to be updated on status changes. Notify monitors your Sent Mail folder and, when the status (delivered, deleted, completed) for a sent message is updated, Notify will alert you.

 Poor Sound? Notify will play most types of Windows sound files. You will need a PC sound card and speakers to use sound files effectively with Notify however.

Check boxes to make notify work

Browse directory button

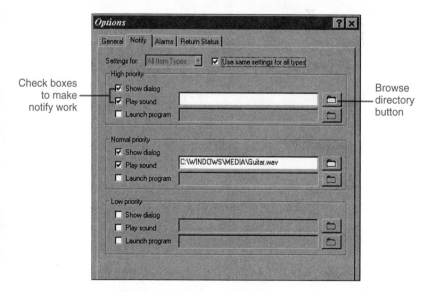

FIGURE 22.4 The Notify tab, where you choose to show a dialog box and play sounds.

7. Once you have chosen the options you want, click OK. Notify will immediately begin monitoring your mailbox for incoming messages.

READING A GROUPWISE 5 MESSAGE USING NOTIFY

When a new message arrives in your mailbox, Notify will alert you. A dialog box will pop up on your computer screen showing you who the message is from and what type of message it is (see Figure 22.5). You will be given the option to **Close** the Notify dialog box, **Read** the message, or **Delete** the message from the Notify dialog box without reading it.

To read the incoming message simply click on the Read button. GroupWise 5 will run and your new message will appear computer screen. You can also right-click the Notify icon on the taskbar and choose **Read** from the quick menu.

 One Notice Only After you read a message, Notify will no longer consider the message new and therefore won't alert you again about the opened message.

A new mail message arrives.

FIGURE 22.5 The Notify alert dialog box.

In this lesson you learned how to start and use Notify, how to change the Notify options and how to read a new message using Notify.

Windows 95 and Windows NT Primer

Windows 95 and Windows NT are graphical operating systems that make your computer easy to use by providing menus and pictures from which you select. Before you can take advantage of either operating system, however, you need to learn some basics that apply to both of them.

Fortunately, Windows 95 and Windows NT operate very much alike. (In fact, they're so similar I'll refer to them both just as Windows throughout the remainder of this appendix.) If the figures you see in this primer don't look exactly like what's on your screen, don't sweat it. Some slight variation may occur depending on your setup, the applications you use, and whether you're on a network. Rest assured, however, that the basic information presented here applies no matter what your setup may be.

A First Look at Windows

You don't really have to start Windows because it starts automatically when you turn on your PC. After the initial startup screens, you arrive at a screen something like the one shown in Figure A.1.

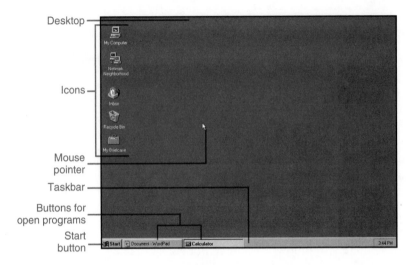

Desktop

Icons

Mouse
pointer

Taskbar

Buttons for
open programs

Start
button

FIGURE A.1   The Windows screen.

PARTS OF THE SCREEN

As you can see, the Windows screen contains a lot of special
elements and controls. Here's a brief summary of those elements:

- The Desktop consists of the background and icons that
  represent programs, tools, and other elements.

- The Taskbar shows a button for each open window and
  program. You can switch between open windows and
  programs by clicking the taskbar button that represents
  the program you want. (The program you are currently
  working in is highlighted in the taskbar.)

- The Start button opens a menu from which you can start
  programs, get help, and find files. To use it, you click the
  Start button, and then you point or click to make a selection from each successive menu that appears. (When you
  point to a selection that has a right-pointing arrow beside
  it, a secondary—or cascading—menu appears.)

- The icons that appear on your desktop give you access to
  certain programs and computer components. You open

an icon by double-clicking it. (An open icon displays a window containing programs, files, or other items.)

• The mouse pointer moves around the screen in relation to your movement of the mouse. You use the mouse pointer to select what you want to work with.

You'll learn more about these elements as you work through the rest of this Windows primer.

TIP

Also Appearing: Microsoft Office   If your computer has Microsoft Office installed on it, the Office Shortcuts toolbar also appears on-screen. It's a series of little pictures strung together horizontally that represent Office programs. Hold the mouse over a picture (icon) to see what it does; click it to launch the program. See your Microsoft Office documentation to learn more.

You may have some other icons on your desktop (representing networks, folders, printers, files, and so on) depending upon what options you chose during initial setup. Double-click an icon to view the items it contains.

USING A MOUSE

To work most efficiently in Windows, you need a mouse. You will perform the following mouse actions as you work:

• **Point**   To position the mouse so that the on-screen pointer touches an item.

• **Click**   To press and release the left mouse button once. Clicking an item usually selects it. Except when you're told to do otherwise (i.e. to right-click), you always use the left mouse button.

TIP   **Southpaw Strategy**   You can reverse these mouse button actions if you want to use the mouse left-handed. To do so, click Start, Settings, Control Panel, and Mouse. Then click the Buttons tab of the Control Panel dialog box and choose Left-handed.

- **Double-click**   To press and release the left mouse button twice quickly. Double-clicking usually activates an item or opens a window, folder, or program. Double-clicking may take some practice because the speed needs to be just right. To change the speed so it better matches your "clicking style," choose Start, Settings, Control Panel, and Mouse. Then click the Buttons tab of the Mouse Properties dialog box and adjust the double-clicking speed so that it's just right for you.

- **Drag**   To place the mouse pointer over the element you want to move, press and hold down the left mouse button, and then move the mouse to a new location. You might drag to move a window, dialog box, or file from one location to another. Except when you're told to do otherwise (i.e. to right-drag), you drag with the left mouse button.

- **Right-click**   To click with the right mouse button. Right-clicking usually displays a shortcut (or pop-up) menu from which you can choose common commands.

Controlling a Window with the Mouse

Ever wonder why the program is called "Windows"? Well, Windows operating systems section off the desktop into rectangular work areas called "windows." These windows are used for particular purposes, such as running a program, displaying options or lists, and so on. Each window has common features used to manipulate the window. Figure A.2 shows how you can use the mouse to control your windows.

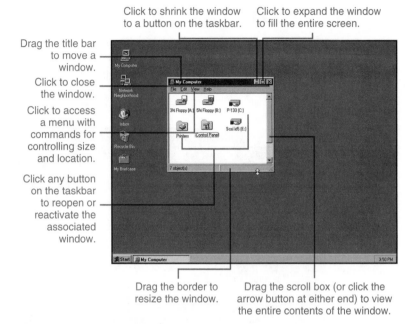

Click to shrink the window to a button on the taskbar.

Click to expand the window to fill the entire screen.

Drag the title bar to move a window.

Click to close the window.

Click to access a menu with commands for controlling size and location.

Click any button on the taskbar to reopen or reactivate the associated window.

Drag the border to resize the window.

Drag the scroll box (or click the arrow button at either end) to view the entire contents of the window.

FIGURE A.2 Use your mouse to control and manipulate windows.

Scrolling for Information If your window contains more information than it can display at once, scroll bars appear on the bottom and/or right edges of the window. To move through the window's contents, click an arrow button at either end of a scroll bar to move in that direction, or drag the scroll box in the direction you want to move.

If you're using the professional version of Office 97, you'll also have enhanced scrolling available to you via your "Intellimouse"—a new mouse by Microsoft that includes a scrolling wheel. Using this mouse is described in all Que books that cover Microsoft Office 97 and its individual applications.

GETTING HELP

Windows comes with a great online Help system. To access it, click the Start button and then click Help. Figure A.3 shows the main Help window with the Contents tab displayed.

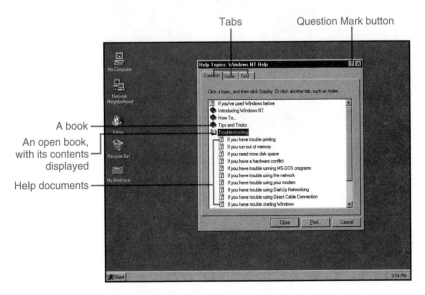

FIGURE A.3 Windows offers several kinds of help.

As you can see here, the Help box contains three tabs (Contents, Index, and Find), each of which provides you with a different type of help. To move to a tab, just click it.

Here's how to use each tab:

- **Contents** Double-click any book to open it and see its sub-books and documents. Double-click a sub-book or document to open it and read the Help topic.

- **Index** When you click this tab, Windows asks you for more information on what you're looking for. Type the word you want to look up, and the Index list scrolls to that part of the alphabetical listing. When you see the topic that you want to read in the list, double-click it.

- **Find**   The first time you click this tab, Windows tells you it needs to create a list. Click Next and then Finish to allow this. When Windows finishes, it asks you to type the word you want to find in the top text box. Then click a word in the middle box to narrow the search. And finally, review the list of Help topics at the bottom and double-click the one you want to read.

When you finish reading about a document, click Help Topics to return to the main Help screen, or click Back to return to the previous Help topic. When you finish with the Help system itself, click the window's Close (X) button to exit.

TIP   **Another Way to Get Help**   In the upper-right corner of the Help window, you should see a question mark next to the Close button. This is (surprise!) the Question Mark button. Whenever you see this button (it appears in other windows besides the Help window), you can click it to change your mouse pointer to a combined arrow-and-question mark. You can then point at any element in the window for a quick "pop-up" description of that element.

Some applications or application suites (such as Microsoft Office 97) may also offer online help. You can learn more about using online help by reading the application's documentation or any Que book that covers the application.

STARTING A PROGRAM

Of the many possible ways to start a program, this is the simplest:

1. Click the Start button.

2. Point to Programs.

3. Click the group that contains the program you want to start (such as **Accessories**).

4. Click the program you want to start (such as **HyperTerminal**).

Figure A.4 shows the series of menus you would go through to start the HyperTerminal application (as suggested in the preceding steps).

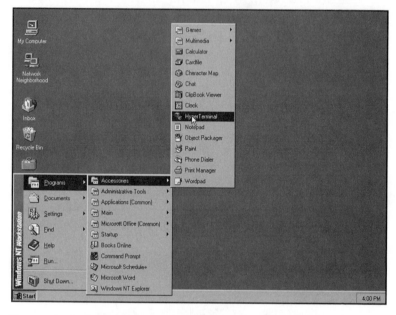

FIGURE A.4   Work through the Start menu and its successive submenus until you find the program you want to start.

Here are a few more ways you can start a program in Windows:

- Open a document that you created in that program. The program automatically opens when the document opens. For example, double-click the My Computer icon on the desktop, find the icon of the document you want to open, and then double-click a document file.

- (Optional) Open a document you created in that program by clicking the Start button, pointing to Programs, and then clicking Windows Explorer. The Windows Explorer window opens; it looks very similar to the File Manager window in Windows 3.1. Locate the directory (or "folder" in Windows 95/NT 4.0 terminology) and double-click the file name. The document opens in the program in which it was created.

- Click the Start button, point to Documents, and select a recently used document from the Documents submenu. Windows immediately starts the program in which you created the file and opens the file.

- If you created a shortcut to the program, you can start the program by double-clicking its shortcut icon on the desktop.

 What's a Shortcut?   Shortcut icons are links to other files. When you use a shortcut, Windows simply follows the link back to the original file. If you find that you use any document or program frequently, you might consider creating a desktop shortcut for it. To do so, just use the right mouse button to drag an object out of Windows Explorer or My Computer and onto the desktop. In the shortcut menu that appears, select Create Shortcut(s) Here.

Using Menus

Almost every Windows program has a menu bar that contains menus. The menu names appear in a row across the top of the screen. To open a menu, click its name (after you click anywhere in the menu bar, you need only point to a menu name to produce the drop-down menu). The menu drops down, displaying its commands (as shown in Figure A.5). To select a command, you simply click it.

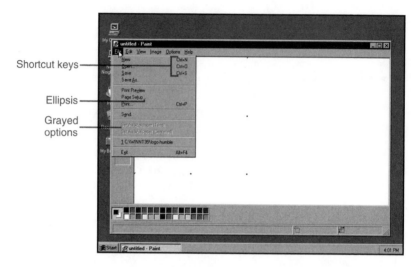

Shortcut keys

Ellipsis

Grayed
options

FIGURE A.5   A menu lists various commands you can perform.

Usually, when you select a command, Windows executes the
command immediately. But you need to keep the following ex-
ceptions to that rule in mind:

- If the command name is gray (instead of black), the command is unavailable in the current situation, and you
  cannot choose it.

- If the command name is followed by an arrow (as the
  selections on the Start menu are), selecting the command
  causes another menu to appear, from which you must
  make another selection.

- If the command is followed by an ellipsis (...), selecting it
  will cause a dialog box to appear. You'll learn about dialog boxes later in this primer.

Shortcut Keys   Key names appear after some command names (for example, Ctrl+O appears to the right of
the Open command, and Ctrl+S appears next to the Save
command). These are shortcut keys, and you can use
them to perform the command without opening the menu.
You should also note that some menu names and commands have one letter underlined. By pressing Alt+the
underlined letter in a menu name, you can open the
menu; by pressing the underlined letter in a command
name, you can select that command from the open menu.

USING SHORTCUT MENUS

A fairly new feature in Windows is the shortcut or pop-up menu.
Right-click any object (any icon, screen element, file, or folder),
and a shortcut menu like the one shown in Figure A.6 appears.
The shortcut menu contains commands that apply only to the
selected object. Click any command to select it, or click outside
the menu to cancel it.

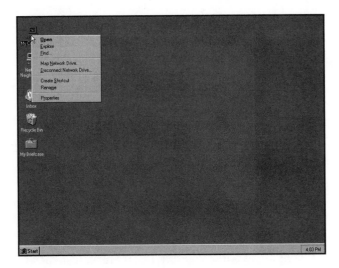

FIGURE A.6   Shortcut menus are new in Windows 95 and
Windows NT 4.0.

NAVIGATING DIALOG BOXES

A dialog box is Windows way of requesting additional information or giving you information. For example, if you choose Print from the File menu of the WordPad application, you see a dialog box something like the one shown in Figure A.7. (The options it displays will vary from system to system.)

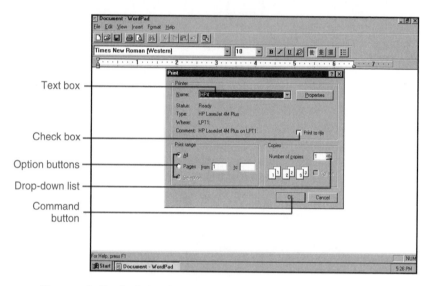

Text box

Check box

Option buttons

Drop-down list

Command button

FIGURE A.7   A dialog box often requests additional information.

Each dialog box contains one or more of the following elements:

- List boxes display available choices. Click any item in the list to select it. If the entire list is not visible, use the scroll bar to see additional choices.

- Drop-down lists are similar to list boxes, but only one item in the list is shown. To see the rest of the list, click the drop-down arrow (to the right of the list box), and then click an item to select it.

- Text boxes allow you to type an entry. Just click inside the text box and type. Text boxes that are designed to hold numbers usually have up and down arrow buttons (called increment buttons) that let you bump the number up and down.

- Check boxes enable you to turn individual options on or off by clicking them. (A check mark or "X" appears when an option is on.)

- Option buttons are like check boxes, except that option buttons appear in groups and you can select only one. When you select an option button, the program automatically deselects whichever one was previously selected. Click a button to activate it, and a black bullet appears inside of the white option circle.

- Command buttons perform an action, such as executing the options you set (OK), canceling the options (Cancel), closing the dialog box, or opening another dialog box. To select a command button, click it.

- Tabs bring up additional "pages" of options you can choose. Click a tab to activate it. (See the section on online help for more information on tabs.)

FROM HERE

If you need more help with Windows, you may want to pick up one of these books:

The Complete Idiot's Guide to Windows 95 by Paul McFedries

Easy Windows 95 by Sue Plumley

The Big Basics Book of Windows 95 by Shelley O'Hara, Jennifer Fulton, and Ed Guilford

Using Windows 95 by Ed Bott

The Complete Idiot's Guide to Windows NT 4.0 Workstation by Paul McFedries

Using Windows NT 4.0 Workstation by Ed Bott

INDEX

H

S

Complete and Return this Card
for a *FREE* Computer Book Catalog

Thank you for purchasing this book! You have purchased a superior computer book written expressly for your needs. To continue to provide the kind of up-to-date, pertinent coverage you've come to expect from us, we need to hear from you. Please take a minute to complete and return this self-addressed, postage-paid form. In return, we'll send you a free catalog of all our computer books on topics ranging from word processing to programming and the internet.

Mr. ☐   Mrs. ☐   Ms. ☐   Dr. ☐

Name (first) ☐☐☐☐☐☐☐☐☐☐ (M.I.) ☐ (last) ☐☐☐☐☐☐☐☐☐☐☐☐☐☐☐

Address ☐☐☐☐☐☐☐☐☐☐☐☐☐☐☐☐☐☐☐☐☐☐☐☐

☐☐☐☐☐☐☐☐☐☐☐☐☐☐☐☐☐☐☐☐☐☐☐☐

City ☐☐☐☐☐☐☐☐☐☐ State ☐☐ Zip ☐☐☐☐☐ ☐☐☐☐

Phone ☐☐☐ ☐☐☐ ☐☐☐☐ Fax ☐☐☐ ☐☐☐ ☐☐☐☐

Company Name ☐☐☐☐☐☐☐☐☐☐☐☐☐☐☐☐☐☐☐☐

E-mail address ☐☐☐☐☐☐☐☐☐☐☐☐☐☐☐☐☐☐☐☐☐☐☐☐☐

1. Please check at least (3) influencing factors for purchasing this book.

Front or back cover information on book .... ☐
Special approach to the content .... ☐
Completeness of content .... ☐
Author's reputation .... ☐
Publisher's reputation .... ☐
Book cover design or layout .... ☐
Index or table of contents of book .... ☐
Price of book .... ☐
Special effects, graphics, illustrations .... ☐
Other (Please specify): _____ ☐

2. How did you first learn about this book?

Internet Site .... ☐
Saw in Macmillan Computer
    Publishing catalog .... ☐
Recommended by store personnel .... ☐
Saw the book on bookshelf at store .... ☐
Recommended by a friend .... ☐
Received advertisement in the mail .... ☐
Saw an advertisement in: _____ ☐
Read book review in: _____ ☐
Other (Please specify): _____ ☐

3. How many computer books have you purchased in the last six months?

This book only .... ☐   3 to 5 books .... ☐
2 books .... ☐   More than 5 .... ☐

4. Where did you purchase this book?

Bookstore .... ☐
Computer Store .... ☐
Consumer Electronics Store .... ☐
Department Store .... ☐
Office Club .... ☐
Warehouse Club .... ☐
Mail Order .... ☐
Direct from Publisher .... ☐
Internet site .... ☐
Other (Please specify): .... ☐

5. How long have you been using a computer?

Less than 6 months .. ☐   6 months to a year ..... ☐
1 to 3 years .... ☐   More than 3 years ...... ☐

6. What is your level of experience with personal computers and with the subject of this book?

	With PC's	With subject of book
New	☐	☐
Casual	☐	☐
Accomplished	☐	☐
Expert	☐	☐

Source Code — ISBN:

7. Which of the following best describes your job title?

Administrative Assistant .... ☐
Coordinator .... ☐
Manager/Supervisor .... ☐
Director .... ☐
Vice President .... ☐
President/CEO/COO .... ☐
Lawyer/Doctor/Medical Professional .... ☐
Teacher/Educator/Trainer .... ☐
Engineer/Technician .... ☐
Consultant .... ☐
Not employed/Student/Retired .... ☐
Other (Please specify): .... ☐

8. Which of the following best describes the area of the company your job title falls under?

Accounting .... ☐
Engineering .... ☐
Manufacturing .... ☐
Marketing .... ☐
Operations .... ☐
Sales .... ☐
Other (Please specify): .... ☐

9. What is your age?

Under 20 .... ☐
21-29 .... ☐
30-39 .... ☐
40-49 .... ☐
50-59 .... ☐
60-over .... ☐

10. Are you:

Male .... ☐
Female .... ☐

11. Which computer publications do you read regularly? (Please list)

_____
_____
_____
_____
_____
_____
_____
_____
_____
_____

Comments: _____
_____
_____

Fold here and scotch-tape to m

l.ll..l.l.l.l...ll.l.l.l.l..l.l.ll.l...ll.l.l.l